Persian
Sufi Poetry

CURZON SUFI SERIES

Series editor: Ian Richard Netton

Professor of Arabic and
Middle Eastern Studies,
University of Leeds

The Curzon Sufi Series attempts to provide short introductions to a variety of facets of the subject, which are accessible both to the general reader and the student and scholar in the field. Each book will be either a synthesis of existing knowledge or a distinct contribution to, and extension of, knowledge of the particular topic. The two major underlying principles of the Series are sound scholarship and readability.

BEYOND FAITH AND INFIDELITY
The Sufi Poetry and Teachings of Mahmud Shabistari
Leonard Lewisohn

AL-HALLAJ
Herbert W. Mason

RUZBIHAN BAQLI
Mysticism and the Rhetoric of Sainthood in Persian Sufism
Carl W. Ernst

ABDULLAH ANSARI OF HERAT
An Early Sufi Master
A.G. Ravan Farhadi

THE CONCEPT OF SAINTHOOD IN EARLY ISLAMIC MYSTICISM
Bernd Radtke and John O'Kane

SUHRAWARDI AND THE SCHOOL OF ILLUMINATION
Mehdi Amin Razavi

R

Persian Sufi Poetry

An Introduction to the Mystical Use of Classical Persian Poems

J.T.P. de Bruijn

CURZON

First Published in 1997
by Curzon Press
St John's Studios, Church Road, Richmond
Surrey, TW9 2QA

Typeset in Horley Old Style by LaserScript Ltd, Mitcham
Printed and bound in Great Britain by
Biddles Limited, Guildford and King's Lynn

British Library Cataloguing in Publication Data
A catalogue record for this book is available from the British Library

ISBN 0–7007–0674–7 (hbk)
ISBN 0–7007–0312–8 (pbk)

Contents

Introduction 1

1 **Mystical Epigrams** 6
Persian quatrains 6
The case of ‘Umar-i Khayyām 9
Bābā Ṭāhir ‘Uryān 13
Shaykh Abū Sa‘īd 16
Bābā Afẕal 19
The *Mukhtār-nāma* of ‘Aṭṭār 21
Anthologies 23
Commentaries 24

2 **Poems of Abstinence** 29
The qaṣīda in secular and religious poetry 29
Kisā’ī 32
Nāṣir-i Khusrau 34
Sanā’ī 35
Sanā’ī’s zuhdīyāt 38
Khāqānī and other 12th century poets of the qaṣīda 43
The qaṣīdas of ‘Aṭṭār 47

3 **Poetry of Love** 51
The theme of love 51
The ghazal as a prosodic form and as a genre 53

The ghazal in the history of literature 54
The scope of ghazal poetry 63
The ghazal as a mystical poem 68
Unbelievers and qalandars 71
A specimen from the ghazal of Ḥāfiẓ 76

4 Teachers and Story-tellers 84
The maṣnavī 84
Didactical poetry 86
The maṣnavīs of Sanā'ī 88
Niẓāmī's Makhzan al-asrār 97
The maṣnavī's of 'Aṭṭār 99
Rūmī's Maṣnavī-yi Ma'navī 108
Sulṭān Valad 111
Sa'dī's Būstān 113
Auḥadī's Jām-i Jam 115
Khvājū Kirmānī 116
Gulshan-i rāz 118
Sufi practices 118
Mystical allegories 121
The Seven Thrones of Jāmī 123

Select Bibliography 128
Index 135

Introduction

The title of this book is the same as the working title which was suggested when I was invited to write it. Now that the writing is done, I do not feel the need to look for a more descriptive name because the provisional title, if correctly understood, expresses almost exactly what the reader will find on the following pages. It tells simply, but clearly enough, that poems will be discussed which were written in the classical Persian language on themes related to the mystical tradition of Islam.

If a few words of explanation are still needed, the reason is, first of all, that the subject thus defined is too extensive to be fully surveyed in a concise volume like this. Since the beginning of the eleventh century AD, the date of the oldest specimens known to us, an enormous amount of mystical poems has been composed in Persian. The poets lived not only in present-day Iran, Afghanistan and Tajikistan, the countries where Persian is at home both as a spoken and a written language, but also in other parts of Asia – in particular the Indian Subcontinent, Central Asia and Turkey – where literary Persian was used for centuries as an important cultural language. Certain limits of time and geography had therefore to be drawn.

Although in the course of this almost millenarian period beautiful and interesting mystical poems have been written at all times and in all places, the history of Persian Sufi poetry has known a 'golden era', as it was called by A.J. Arberry, whose

Classical Persian Literature covers the same period as the present survey.[1] The greatest Sufi poets who created the most influential poems all lived during a period roughly corresponding to the European Middle Ages. As a convenient final date 1492 was chosen, the year when Mullā 'Abd ar-Raḥmān Jāmī died, a great Sufi sheikh as well as a very productive writer, whose mystical poetry provided suitable material to conclude each of the four chapters of this book.

Shortly after Jāmī's death the Safavids united the greater part of the Persian homelands under their rule. This political incident greatly changed the religious and cultural climate, notably through the introduction of Shi'ite Islam as the national religion of the country we now know as Iran. Classical Persian literature survived all this and, up to the present century, continued to be the most conspicuous element of the Persian cultural identity. It was even strong enough to penetrate the civilisations of other Asian nations. From the sixteenth century onwards Indian and Turkish Muslims participated increasingly in the tradition of Persian poetry, not only by writing in Persian but also by following the examples set by the poets of Persia in their own languages. During the 'medieval' period these developments had hardly begun. On the whole, the poets reviewed here were Sunni Muslims and nearly all lived, or at least were born, in the lands where Persian language was the indigenous language.

In its earliest form, the Persian language appears in the cuneiform inscriptions of the Achaemenian Kings of Kings written between the sixth and fourth centuries BC. After the destruction of the Old Persian empire by Alexander the Great, it disappeared from historical records for several centuries until, from the third century AD onwards, it was adopted again as a literary medium (called Middle Persian or Pahlavi) by Sasanian kings, Zoroastrians and Manichaeans. In the seventh century, when the Arabs brought the religion of Islam to Persia, another major break occurred in the continuity of Persian culture. Arabic became the exclusive medium of literary culture in the dominating Muslim community. However, already in the second half of the ninth century, Persian began to be used in writing again in the eastern provinces of the Abbasid caliphate. Political circumstances which brought rulers of local origin into power, favoured the rapid development of a New Persian language. In many ways it was a typical product of the civilisation of Islam: the script, a large section of the vocabulary and many literary forms were derived from Arabic. Moreover, the latter language remained an important factor in Persian culture, where it continued to play more or less the same rôle as Latin did in medieval Europe. Arabic was particularly dominant in the religious disciplines, one of which was the 'science of Sufism'.

Until the twentieth century, when it was significantly modernised under Western influence, Persian poetry was a highly formalised artistic tradition. To write a poem meant, in the first place, to apply certain unchangeable rules covering prosody, imagery and the use of rhetorical devices. A basic rule of prosody was that each poem should be constructed as a sequence of distichs or *bayts*. The two half-verses of each distich are virtually identical as far as their metrical patterns are concerned. The rhyme is either internal (a-a) or only final (b-a), linking the line with the other distichs of the poem. The former marks the distich as an opening line, if the poem is a lyric; the latter could be used in any other line. In this way, most verse forms current in the tradition can be defined. The most important are the quatrain or *rubā'ī*, the *qaṣīda*, the *ghazal* and the *masnavī*. To each of these four verse forms one of the chapters in this book will be devoted.

Initially, this poetry was almost entirely a matter of the medieval Persian courts and therefore essentially a secular tradition. The characteristic form was the *qaṣīda*, which was most often used for poems of praise. When the Sufis began to write Persian poems they adapted many forms of court poetry to their own ends. Sufi poetry retained several traces of this origin; the distinction with secular poetry is therefore sometimes difficult to make. On the other hand, the remarkable expansion of Sufi poetry equally made its impact on the poetry of 'the world' so that eventually the lines distinguishing the two became vague. This caused serious problems for the interpretation of Persian poetry, especially as far as the lyrical genre of the *ghazal* is concerned.

The controversy surrounding the mystical or non-mystical readings of Ḥāfiẓ's poetry is the most typical example.

A mystical trend must have been present in Islam from the very beginning. The English word Sufism, as Islamic mysticism is usually referred to, was derived from the Arabic *taṣavvuf* which, according to the most likely explanation, originally meant 'to don a woollen cloak'. It would then refer to the predominance, during the first few centuries, of ascetic piety, influenced, as it seems, by the practices of Christian hermits in the Syrian desert. Accounts of the acts and the sayings of the early sheikhs are preserved in an extensive hagiographical literature, written in Arabic and Persian. Already in the eighth century (the second of the Islamic era) more reflective books appeared, which mark the beginnings of a rich flowering of Sufi literature in prose and poetry composed over the centuries in every cultural language of the Islamic world. These works cover the various aspects of mystical experience and ethics as well as metaphysical theory as, from the late twelfth century onwards, it developed out of a merger of philosophy and Sufism; the most influential body of mystical doctrine was Muḥyī ad-Dīn Ibn al-'Arabī's theosophy known as the thesis of *waḥdat al-wujūd* the 'Unity of Being'.

The first Sufi poets about whom we have any knowledge were Arabs. Love poetry of great intensity has been attributed to the great mystics, such as the poetess Rābi'a of Basra (d. 801), the Egyptian saint Dhū'n-Nūn (d. 861) and al-Ḥallāj of Baghdad (executed in 922) whom the Persian poets celebrated as the prime example of sacrifice for love's sake under the name 'Manṣūr'.[2] When in the eleventh century Persian Sufis started to write and read poetry, they continued a long-standing practice. The Persians, however, were able to create a lasting and extremely fertile tradition, whereas Arabic literature of later centuries produced few mystical poets of any importance besides Ibn al-Fāriḍ (d. 1235) and Ibn al-'Arabī (d. 1240) who wrote the mystical love poems collected in *Tarjumān al-ashwāq*.[3]

The size of this volume makes it impossible to include an introduction to Sufism. For this, the reader should turn to one of the works mentioned in the Select Bibliography. The focus of our attention will be the reflections of mysticism in Persian poetry. Reynold Nicholson's statement that 'Ṣūfiism has few ideas, but an inexhaustible wealth and variety of illustration'[4] is no longer tenable since our knowledge of Sufi literature has expanded greatly since the end of the nineteenth century. Yet, there might still be some truth in this claim if we restrict it to Sufi poetry in particular. The mystical concepts one needs to be familiar with in order to understand the words of the poets are comparatively few. Many of them concern general items of religious ethics rather than intricate points of esoteric doctrine. The brief explanations given in the course of the exposition will probably be enough for the reader who has only a general knowledge of Sufi ideas. The translated specimens will also speak for themselves in most cases.

Throughout this survey, the emphasis will be on the poems rather than on the poets. As a rule, biographical information is used to elucidate poetry, not the other way round. Such data are inserted at those places where they best fit in with the main line of argument, which need not be the first instance of mentioning the name of a particular poet. Within each chapter a chronological order is followed. In Chapter 3, on the *ghazal*, which is mostly of an analytical nature, the history of the genre is discussed in a separate section.

Being an introduction, the main purpose of this book is to show the way to the vast literature available to those who wish to acquire a deeper knowledge of the subject. Readers should seek help from the Select Bibliography and the references contained in the Notes.

Notes

1. CPL, p. 450.
2. His name was really al-Ḥusayn ibn Manṣūr al-Ḥallāj. On Arabic mystical poetry see in particular A. Schimmel, *As Through a Veil*, pp. 11–48.
3. Edited and translated by Reynold A. Nicholson, London 1911.
4. *Selected poems from the Dīvāni Shamsi Tabrīz*, Cambridge 1898, p. viii.

1

Mystical Epigrams

Persian quatrains

Nearly all *dīvāns* of Persian poets contain, besides poems in the great classical forms, collections of shorter poems. Among the latter, some are irregular pieces (at least from the point of view of standard prosody), of various lengths, but usually not longer than a few lines, which are called 'fragments' (*qiṭ'as* or *muqaṭṭa'āt*). Although this term does not necessarily imply that these poems are unfinished or incomplete, they do in fact have a rather informal character. Such 'fragments' often served as occasional poems or epigrams, and are therefore much closer to the day-to-day practice of poetry than the more finished *qaṣīdas* and *ghazals*. Only rarely did they gain more importance, as for instance in the poetry of Ibn-i Yamīn (1286–1368),[1] a court poet of the Mongol period, whose output of fragmentary poems was considerable both in quantity and in substance. His muqaṭṭa'āt express philosophical and ethical reflections, mostly based on nothing more profound than worldly wisdom and common sense. However, occasionally mystical ideas can be found as well. Whether this justifies the qualification of Ibn-i Yamīn as a Sufi poet is still a matter of debate, which is complicated by the fact that sometimes his poetry was confused with that of an outspoken mystical poet of the sixteenth century, who happened to be his namesake.

Among the shorter poems another form, the quatrain, played a much greater part in Sufi poetry than the *muqaṭṭaʻāt*. As far as our present knowledge goes, it was the earliest kind of poetry that was read and written by Persian mystics. Literary history, therefore, indicates that we should begin our survey with the quatrains, but, apart from that consideration, they also provide a good starting point for a discussion of some of the basic features of this tradition.

Persian quatrains are poems of four lines with, most often, a rhyme pattern a-a/b-a, although among the earliest specimens known to us the sequence of two internal rhymes (a-a/a-a) also frequently occurs. If it is described in terms of the general principles of Persian prosody, a quatrain of the type a-a/b-a can also be defined as a very brief poem of two distichs. Actually, the term *du-baytī* (literally, a poem 'of two distichs') has been in use, but only for quatrains which deviate from the metrical rules for a regular quatrain. Another term, sometimes applied to quatrains, is *tarāna*, properly denoting a 'song' or a 'melody' and referring to the musical use of quatrains. The most common appellation of a Persian quatrain is *rubāʻī* (with the plural *rubāʻīyāt*), a derivation from the Arabic numeral *arbaʻ* ('four'). A remarkable feature of this name is that, contrary to Persian prosodical theory, the four lines, or 'half verses', are counted here as separate entities.[2]

This is not the only deviation from standard prosody. The Persian rubāʻī also has a metre of its own, which cannot be fitted into the patterns of metrical theory, although it is, like all other Persian metres, based on quantity, that is the distinction between short and long syllables. The pattern of the rubāʻī is a sequence of twenty metrical units, called *mora* in metrical theory. In some places of the sequence only long syllables (equivalent to two *moras*) can be used, but in others one long syllable may be replaced by two short ones so that the actual number of syllables in a line may vary between ten and thirteen. This variety gave the rubāʻī a great measure of flexibility, which may have been one of the reasons for its immense popularity.

According to Shams-i Qays, who in the early thirteenth century wrote the most comprehensive exposition of Persian prosody, the rubāʻī was invented by the poet Rūdakī (fl. tenth century). He would have derived its metrical pattern from a rhythmical phrase shouted by a playing child and then adapted it to the rules of classical prosody. Although it gives only a legendary explanation of the origin, the anecdote does betray an awareness of the non-classical nature of the rubāʿī metre. The true origin remains unknown in spite of attempts to prove that the rubāʿī was derived either from Persian popular literature or from early Turkish poetry where quatrains were quite common, although not in quantitative but rather in syllabic metrics. Whatever the case may be, it is very likely that quatrains initially belonged to a literary stratum distinct from the realm of polite poetry which produced the classical forms.

The quatrain is most often an epigram, the terse formulation of a poetical idea, suitable to serve as a brief interruption in a conversation, a sermon or a prose composition. Because of the great variety of its uses, it is impossible to delimit the subject-matter of the quatrain. Rubāʿīs deal with any theme that could be treated in classical Persian poetry. Particular to them is a pithy and pointed mode of expression, using wit and striking images in order to enforce and illustrate the poet's statement. To be successful the poem has to express a certain development of thought, for which in many cases the third non-rhyming line is used. It connects the initial idea or image put forward in the first two lines to a conclusion contained in the final line. This structural feature made the quatrain into an important medium for maxims, which may convey mere secular wisdom but also profound religious ideas.

To a certain extent, quatrains are comparable to the individual distichs of longer poems, which often show a similar epigrammatical structure. The difference is, however, that quatrains always stand on their own, without any connection whatsoever to a larger poetic structure. Their actual meaning depended very much upon the context in which the poem was presented. This context could be a literary text as well as oral speech; in the latter case, such contexts usually have left no traces and this seriously limits the possibility of drawing conclusions from quatrains with regard to the ideas they express. This point should be kept in mind, especially when one tries to read quatrains as statements of Sufi doctrine.

Generally speaking, the classical Persian tradition is one of individualised authorship. Poems of other kinds, whether lyrics or epics, are usually firmly connected to specific names. Although there are indeed cases of flagrant literary mystifications known concerning these verse forms, this does not contradict the fact that, on the whole, the concept of an individual author prevails throughout the Persian tradition.

The case of 'Umar-i Khayyām

Again, the Persian quatrains are a different case. This has become particularly clear in the remarkable instance of 'Umar Khayyām's collection of quatrains, which to most Western readers constitutes the epitome of Persian poetry. In Persia itself, 'Umar was not much regarded as a poet until his worldwide fame began to spread from Victorian England through the amazing success of Edward FitzGerald's adaptation of 'Umar's quatrains in his poem 'The Rubâiyât of Omar Khayyâm'. It was first published in 1859, reprinted many times and translated into all the major languages of the world.[3]

During his lifetime, 'Umar-i Khayyām (1048–1131) was a celebrated scholar, not only in philosophy and the sciences but also in theology. The only writings attributable with certainty to him are in Arabic on the subjects of mathematics, astronomy and metaphysics. All that we know about 'Umar's life points to a more or less normal existence as a distinguished medieval scholar, who found patrons among the rulers and other influential men of his days. The earliest reference to him as a poet occurs in 'Imād ad-Dīn Iṣfahānī's *Kharīdat al-qaṣr,* an anthology of Arabic poetry, and some other Arabic writers of the late twelfth century who cite a few short poems of his. That Khayyām, like any other cultured person, would have written Arabic poetry occasionally, is not unusual, and it is even quite possible that at times he may have improvised some Persian quatrains. However, considering the lack of any documentary evidence to the contrary, it is extremely unlikely that his poetic output was significant in quantity or that any single poem attributed to him may ever be proved to be authentic.

Towards the end of the twelfth century, the theologian Fakhr ad-Dīn Rāzī (d. 1210) for the first time cited a single Persian quatrain under his name. The same poem, together with another one, can be found in a well-known Sufi textbook, the *Mirṣād al-'ibād min al-mabda' ilā'l-ma'ād* by Najm ad-Dīn Dāya, written about 1223. It was not until the fourteenth century that anthologists were able to assemble small collections of Khayyām's quatrains: in Jājarmī's *Mu'nis al-aḥrār* (1339–40) thirteen poems have been preserved, and the anonymous collector of *Nuzhat al-majālis* (1330) could bring together thirty-one poems. It is remarkable that several of these early specimens occur in more than one of the sources. This points to the existence of only a very limited corpus of quatrains ascribed to Khayyām prior to the fifteenth century. The famous manuscript of the Bodleian Library, compiled in 1460, which was used by FitzGerald, contains 158 poems; but in the anthology *Ṭarabkhāna*, compiled only two years later, already 554 rubā'īyāt were brought together. This number increased even more in later collections of Khayyām's quatrains.

Stimulated by the outburst of public interest in these quatrains, Orientalists began to examine the problems of the textual transmission. An amazing outcome of this research was that, in 1897, Vladimir Zhukovsky, a professor at the University of St. Petersburg, showed that a great number of the poems which circulated under the name of Khayyām could be attributed in medieval manuscripts to other poets as well. Thus a substantial group of poems were identified as 'wandering quatrains', that is poems of multiple attribution, the true authorship of which is impossible to establish.[4]

It has become clear that there exists no such thing as a stable corpus of these quatrains. The findings in the earliest sources do not provide an absolute certainty that any of the cited poems were really by Khayyām. Even if they are genuine, there are not enough poems found in these sources to allow the reconstruction of his poetic personality. If these facts are acknowledged, we are forced to redefine Khayyām's place in the history of Persian literature. As a poet he seems to have been the creation of a collective imagination rather than a literary figure to be held responsible for the thoughts expressed in the quatrains. A more realistic view of his place in the history of Persian literature is that he became the eponym of a cluster of poetic themes exemplified in numerous poems whose real authors remained anonymous. The poetic *persona* speaking in these quatrains might be described as a world-famous scientist and metaphysician who, at the end of a life spent in an endeavour to grasp the rationale behind the universe, is resigned to doubting the ability of the human mind to solve the enigmas presented by this world and by man's transitory existence on earth.[5]

The question which needs to be answered with regard to our focus of interest is whether or not this poetic *persona* of Khayyām is in any way connected with Sufi poetry. This has been another issue concerning our poet-scholar which became the subject of a heated debate, even earlier than the authenticity of the quatrains. The first Western translator to defend a mystical interpretation of Khayyām's quatrains was J.B. Nicolas, who had lived in Persia as a French consul. He based his translation (published in 1867) on a lithographed edition containing a collection of 464 quatrains. His view contradicted the interpretation of Edward FitzGerald who had presented Khayyām as a sceptic seeking a remedy for his disillusion with the world and with his own intellect in a *carpe-diem* philosophy. Nicolas' version of the poems met with much less success than FitzGerald's; nevertheless, his mystical reading has always found its followers. It was defended for the last time in 1967 by the English poet Robert Graves in the introduction to a volume of translations, which were soon proven to be founded on forged material.[6] The least that could be said in favour of Nicolas' point of view is that it did have an authentic background in so far as it was based on the teaching of a Sufi of Tehran, who had explained Khayyām's poems to the translator.[7] Apparently, the quatrains were indeed susceptible to a genuine mystical interpretation, and this need not surprise because themes like the vanity of the world, the transcience of life, or the insufficiency of human reason in solving the world's mysteries, are in themselves quite compatible with a mystical outlook and were commonplace in genuine Sufi poetry.

The earliest references by mystics to Khayyām, however, speak a different language. Among the very first specimens of the Khayyām corpus on record are the two poems cited by the mystical writer Najm ad-Dīn Dāya:

The circle of our coming and our going
Has no beginning and shall have no end.
No one can ever in this world explain
Whence was this coming and to where the going.

The Keeper Who arranged this complex body
Why did He bring it to decay and ruin?
Was it an ugly form? Who is to blame?
Or was it good? Who would destroy it then?

Dāya's quotations were intended as a disapproval and were accompanied by a sharp condemnation of the false doctrines of philosophers like 'Umar-i Khayyām, who only reckoned with the forces of Fate and Nature, but ignored the sublime states to which the mystics aspire.[8]

In a similar spirit the great Sufi poet Farīd ad-Dīn 'Aṭṭār (d.ca. 1220) made use of an anecdote concerning 'Umar's fate after his death. In his didactical poem *Ilāhī-nāma* ('The Book of the Divine') he tells about a clairvoyant who, standing at Khayyām's grave, saw him in a 'state of imperfection': 'Umar was bathing in his sweat for shame and confusion. As the clairvoyant explained, he had boasted at the Heavenly Gate of his learning but was deeply embarrassed when he learned how ignorant he really was.[9]

Quatrains were commonly put to the names of other famous scholars and mystics, some of whom lived even earlier than Khayyām. The great philosopher Abū 'Alī ibn-i Sīnā, known to the West as Avicenna (d. 1037), is also accredited with a number of short Persian poems, including quatrains. Some of the Sufi sheikhs who are mentioned as the authors of quatrains are 'Abd Allāh Anṣārī of Herat (d. 1089) and Abū'l-Ḥasan Kharaqānī (d. 1033). All these attributions are very uncertain.

Bābā Ṭāhir 'Uryān

The problems concerning the authorship of quatrains supposed to have been written in the eleventh century are particularly relevant to our discussion, because they concern the dating of the very beginning of Persian Sufi poetry. For all we know, the quatrain was the first verse form which the mystics used for the expression of their thoughts and experiences. Unfortunately, to all specimens known from the eleventh century the philological uncertainties just outlined are attached.

If we may trust the single chronological indication about his life, the first Sufi who can be identified individually as a poet would have been Bābā Ṭāhir, nicknamed 'Uryān ('the Naked').[10] At some time between 1055 and 1058 Sultan Ṭughril Beg, who had just established the Saljuq House as the new Turkish power in the eastern part of the Abbasid Caliphate, made his entry in the city of Hamadan. Three Sufi saints were standing on a hill near the gate. 'The Sultán's eyes fell upon them; he halted the vanguard of his army, alighted, approached, and kissed their hands.' One of them, who was 'somewhat crazy in his manner' said to Ṭughril: 'O Turk, what wilt thou do with God's people?.' The pious man who thus dared to remind the new ruler of his duty as the protector of the community of the believers, was Bābā Ṭāhir.[11]

The date of this event conflicts with a dating of Bābā Ṭāhir's death in the Muslim year 410 (1019–20) given by the nineteenth century anthologist Riẓā-Qulī Khān Hidāyat, which is not supported by any earlier source. There remains, inevitably, a considerable doubt regarding the dating of his life, and no other biographical details are available. On the other hand, the few facts that are known all point to Hamadan as his hometown, or possibly the nearby mountains of Luristan. In that area he was immortalised by the Ahl-i Ḥaqq ('The People of the Truth'), a sect beyond the farthest boundaries of Islamic heterodoxy with a following among the Lurs of the Zagros mountains. In their sacred book *Saranjām*, Bābā Ṭāhir appears as an angel serving the third of the seven manifestations of the Divine who made their appearance in the sacred history of the world according to the mythology of the Ahl-i Ḥaqq.

As a literary figure, Bābā Ṭāhir is more tangible because of the works attributed to him. They include a fairly large amount of quatrains and a few *ghazal*s. The former deviate from the standard rubā'īyāt because they are written in one of the variations of the *hazaj*, which is a common metre in classical poetry. Another particularity pertains to the language of these quatrains which, although written basically in literary Persian, contain many dialect forms. It has been argued that they were originally composed in the Luri dialect and in the course of time were more and more adapted to the standard language.[12] To distinguish these poems from the regular quatrains they are often referred to as *du-baytī*s. There also exists a collection of 400 Arabic maxims on Sufi themes, entitled *al-Kalimāt al-qiṣār* ('The brief words'), on which a number of commentaries, both in Arabic and Persian, have been written.

To add to the obscurity surrounding the historical figure of Bābā Ṭāhir there are uncertainties with regard to the authenticity of the quatrains. The oldest source which contains a few of these poems dates from the fifteenth century; the other poems can be found only in much later collections. The *du-baytī*s are still very popular in Persia. An album compiled by Vaḥīd Dastgirdī in 1927, which contains 256 quatrains considered to be genuine by the editor, was reprinted many times over.

It is hardly possible to attach historical value to the image of Bābā Ṭāhir's personality as it is reflected in these poems, and the same applies to the mystical ideas expressed. The collection has without doubt been added to later, so that mystical concepts and symbols have been inserted which were still strange to a rural saint of the eleventh century.

With these reservations in mind, it should be said that the image we gain from this uncertain source has a number of traits which lend it a remarkable individuality. Bābā Ṭāhir appears to us as a dervish, the wandering beggar for the sake of his mystical search:

While I wander through the desert, night and day,
Tears are streaming from my eyes, night and day.
No fever do I feel, nor pain in any place;
I only know that I am crying, night and day.

Occasionally, terms are used which belong to the vocabulary of the *qalandars*, a phenomenon which appeared only more than a century later in the history of Sufism. It did play a great part in the development of Sufi poetry, but this also was a development which had not yet begun in the lifetime of Bābā Ṭāhir.[13]

I am that drunk whom they call a 'qalandar';
I have no home, no family, no shelter.
My days I spend circling your place;
At night I put my head upon the tiles.

Bābā Ṭāhir presents himself in particular as a desperate lover whose outbursts of passion have a prominent place on his repertoire. His love is often expressed in a quite profane manner but the true intention cannot be mistaken if we take into account the meaning of the corpus as a whole.

Your locks are these two strings on my robab;
Why do you keep me in such wretched state?
At all times you refuse to be with me;
Why are you entering my dreams at night?

Love means above all loneliness and suffering because the object of his yearning remains unattainable.

My Lord, take care of my lonely heart!
Friend of the friendless! I am friendless.
They say: 'Poor Ṭāhir does not have a friend'.
The One I love is God; do I need any friend?

There is a passionate gloom in many of these quatrains, when they speak of the continuing fight against the soul that clings to this world; this struggle can only end in the final destruction of the 'self', the most formidable obstacle on the path towards the Beloved. In one of Bābā Ṭāhir's quatrains physical death is welcomed as the delivery of the soul from its bondage to this world:

That great day when the grave shall hold me tight,
My head will rest on tiles and mud and stones.
The feet turned to the Qiblah, the soul set free,
My body will be in a fight with snakes and ants.

Shaykh Abū Sa'īd

The second collection of early Sufi quatrains ascribed to a mystic who lived in the eleventh century contains rubā'īyāt of the regular kind. In this case, the historical setting of the poems is quite clear, at least as far as the personality of the assumed poet is concerned. Abū Sa'īd ibn Abī'l-Khayr of Mayhana (967–1049) was one of the greatest mystics of his age, and exerted a strong personal influence on the Sufi tradition, especially in his native Khurasan. There is in existence a rich documentation of his life and teaching. His tradition lived on among his family, as it appears from two important descriptions of his life which were composed by his descendants. The first, entitled *Ḥālāt va sukhanān-i Shaykh Abū Sa'īd ibn Abī'l-Khayr* ('The Life and Sayings of . . .'), was written about a century after his death by an anonymous relative. This short hagiography provided the basis for a much more elaborate work, *Asrār at-tauḥīd fī maqāmāt ash-shaykh Abī Sa'īd* ('The Secrets of Unification on the Stages of the Shaykh Abū Sa'īd') by Muḥammad ibn al-Munavvar, another member of his family, who wrote about the middle of the twelfth century. On the basis of these and several other sources, comprehensive studies have been devoted to Abū Sa'īd's mysticism.[14]

The quatrains are the only texts purported to be composed by Abū Sa'īd himself. Again, however, the problem of the authenticity of this attribution is hard to solve. The collections of these quatrains to be found in modern publications have been assembled from a great number of sources, some of which are of a rather recent date. Moreover, it is by no means certain that Abū Sa'īd did compose any quatrains at all. Ibn al-Munavvar states very clearly that the Master did not have time for composing any poetry, as he was preoccupied by his mystical ecstacies. Elsewhere in the same work, his grandson is quoted as saying that Abū Sa'īd composed only one quatrain and a single line of poetry. All the poems that he used in his teaching and his discourses were cited from the sayings of his spiritual directors, in particular his first teacher, Bishr-i Yāsīn. In a story relating how Abū Sa'īd as a boy came in touch with the life of the mystics, a quatrain does indeed play a major part. When his father took him to a gathering of his friends, who once a week used to come together to perform prayers and indulge in a session of *samā'*, that is 'listening' to music and poetry, he heard a *qavvāl* ('singer') recite this poem:

This love of suffering is a gift to the derwishes;
To be killed is to them the essence of holiness;
Dinars and dirhams do not give people any worth;
To the right people only a soul sacrified has a value.

When the singer had recited these lines, a state of ecstacy came upon the derwishes. They danced the whole night until the morning on these verses continuing to be in an excited mood. The singer repeated the verses so often that the Master learned them by heart. When he came home he asked his father to tell him what they meant. 'Be silent !', his father said, 'If you cannot grasp their meaning, why bother about them?' Later, when his father had died already, Abū Sa'īd often quoted the poem in the course of his conversations. He then added: 'Today I would have to say to my father, "At that time you did not know yourself what you heard!"'.[15]

If we give full credit to the reports in the *Asrār at-tauḥīd*, which in spite of its many hagiographical traits is still the best informed source available on the life of Abū Sa'īd, the view that he was himself a poet of *rubā'īyāt* has to be abandoned. On the other hand, we may accept as historical fact that in his time Persian poems, in particular quatrains, were indeed currently used in the circles of mystics and probably played a major part in their spiritual exercises. The repertoire of singers, like the one who performed at the occasion related by Ibn al-Munavvar, could best be described as a pool of poetic material brought together from a variety of authors who remained anonymous. This corpus of poems could easily be supplemented in later times and circulate, originally in an oral tradition and subsequently in the form of collected albums of very heterogeneous contents.

It then becomes understandable why the collection attributed to Abū Sa'īd contains such a variety of themes and images. Already Hermann Ethé, the German scholar who in the nineteenth century collected for the first time the scattered quatrains of Abū Sa'īd from Persian anthologies, observed that the entire range of subjects and symbols familiar from Sufi poetry could already be found in these poems. To Ethé, this meant that Abū Sa'īd was the actual founder of this tradition because, in most cases, he accepted the authenticity of the ascriptions given by his sources. However, Nicholson's evaluation of the problem is undoubtedly nearer to the mark:

> *[the collected quatrains] form a miscellaneous anthology drawn from a great number of poets who flourished at different periods, and consequently they reflect the typical ideas of Persian mysticism as a whole.*[16]

The following examples, all to be found in twelfth century sources, though only seldom attributed to Abū Sa'īd in so many words, cannot give more than a glimpse of this variegated corpus at an early stage of its development. Expressions of mystical love are well represented. They include statements of the identification with the Divine Beloved leading to the effacement of self:

I have my eyes filled by the vision of the Beloved.
My eyes rejoice when the Beloved is there.
Between eye and Beloved one cannot distinguish:
He is in the eye, or the eye is nothing else but He.

My body became all tears and my eyes wept.
Loving you, one should live without a body.
No trace remained of me; why is there Love?
Now I became the Beloved entirely, where is the Lover?

When I shall be dead for twenty years or more,
Do you think that my grave holds no love anymore ?
When you touch the ground and ask: Who lies here?
You will hear a voice crying out: How is my Beloved?

However, one also meets with utterances of a much more submissive piety, which emphasises the sufferings of the loving mystic and the duties incumbent upon him rather than his privileged ecstacies:

Oh the pain of always having to face the road!
Of having to fold this lover's bed again!
Do not regard your piety, all your good works,
Only consider His compassion and His grace!

Do not seek the gardens of Heaven without serving God.
Do not seek Solomon's empire without the seal of belief.
If you want to acquire the possession of both worlds,
Do not seek anything that might hurt a Muslim's heart.[17]

Bābā Afz̤al

Even as late as the Mongol period (thirteenth–fourteenth century), another corpus of quatrains became attached to the name of a great mystical philosopher. Afz̤al ad-Dīn Kāshī, or Maraqī, who is also known as Bābā Afz̤al, was probably a contemporary of the famous Shi'ite scholar and scientist Naṣīr ad-Dīn Ṭūsī (1200–73), but this is the only piece of information about his life which can help us to date him. Several of his prose works have survived. They deal mainly with philosophical subjects in the Aristotelian tradition. Bābā Afẓal also wrote on religious matters, notably on Sufism, and seems to have been influenced by the ideas of the Ismā'īlī's, although he was probably a Sunni Muslim. The quatrains attributed to the name of Bābā Afẓal were collected for the first time by S. Nafīsī, who brought together no fewer than 493 poems from many sources which are all very late, however. The only medieval source containing poetry by Bābā Afẓal is the anthology *Mu'nis al-aḥrār* by Jājarmī (1341), but here we find only a group of *ghazals*. In a more recent collection the number of quatrains is reduced to 195 poems[18]

In the following quatrains, which are among the most frequently ascribed to Afẓal, the poet speaks on a predominantly homiletic note:

Come back! Come back! Whatever you are, come back!
Unbeliever, worshipper of Fire or Idol, come back!
Our gateway is not a gateway of despair;
Though vows were broken a hundred times, come back!

The sweets of this world are less than our dry bread;
The brocate of the world is our woollen habit.
What is this talk of the Cup that Shows the World?
A hundred such cups can you find in this breast.

The one you envy will become your ruler;
The one to whom you show no anger your prisoner.
Give a helping hand as much as you can;
The hand you hold will also hold yours.

The heart cries out for power in this world
And yearns to extend this life eternally.
Poor creature, knowing not that at its heels
The Hunter of Death is out for its life.

The *Mukhtār-nāma* of 'Aṭṭār

The rubā'ī is not always a poem of questionable authorship. There are quatrains to be found in the collected works of practically all the great masters of the Sufi tradition who will be mentioned in the course of the following chapters of the present survey. The oldest of these collections incorporated in a *dīvān* is the set of quatrains of Sanā'ī of Ghazna (d. 1131). Among the many poets of quatrains mention should be made at least of Jalāl ad-Dīn Rūmī, Auḥad ad-Dīn Kirmānī (thirteenth century) and 'Abd ar-Raḥmān Jāmī (fifteenth century).

More than passing attention must be given to the rubā'īyāt of Farīd ad-Dīn 'Aṭṭār (died about 1220), who especially became famous for his mystical epics. His poetical output is, however, more varied than is usually known to Western readers and includes, besides a substantial *Dīvān*, also a separate volume of quatrains. As the title of the collection, *Mukhtār-nāma* ('Book of Selection') indicates the work contains merely an anthology by the poet from his quatrains, which he made because they were too numerous to be included in the *Dīvān*.[19] In an introduction he thus explains the spiritual values to be found in his *rubā'īyāt*:

> *These verses are the result of experiences; there is nothing artificial about them and they are free from any pretence. I wrote them down as they came to me and entered my blood. If one day actual experience gets your soul in its grip, and if you, for some nights, have been submerged in confusion, then you will know from which nest these tender nightingales and these sweet-talking parrots flew: 'Whoever did not taste it, will never know.'*

Quite remarkable is the division of the collection into fifty chapters, each containing quatrains devoted to a specific theme. The classification is a very fine one. It not only includes a detailed list of religious and mystical subjects, but also motifs and images current in Persian lyrical poetry: the description of a beloved person and the sufferings of the lover, antinomian attitudes and wine drinking, the rose, dawn and the celebrated simile of the moth and the candle. The following examples show the variety of 'Aṭṭār's repertoire:

You think that you can see the soul?
Behold all secrets hidden in the world?
The more your vision is perfected,
The more your blindness comes to light.[20]

I said: For your sake I put heart and soul at risk.
All things that I possessed I sacrified to you.
He said: Who are you that you should do or do not?
It was no one but me who robbed you from your rest.[21]

The Christian boy who made me break my vow,
Last night he came and made me touch his locks.
After he danced around four times he left me
Bound four turns to the girdle of his unbelief.[22]

To the rose I spoke: You are like Kanaan's Joseph;
The sultanate of meadow's Egypt suits you well.
The pages of my petals are so many, the rose said,
It is only one of these that you can read.[23]

Oh dawn! When you'll begin to rise,
You will set out to seek my death.
If my heart's sighs should really hurt you,
Only halfway you would turn and go back.[24]

Thus moth to candle spoke: Be my beloved!
The candle said: If you so madly love me,
Enter my flame; and be consumed by it
If you so badly want to be embraced.[25]

Being aware of the discrepancy between imagery and meaning in many of these quatrains, 'Aṭṭār apologises for having devoted so much attention to subjects which might seem to be frivolous and unworthy of his lofty intentions:

*If the reader through determined meditation reaches the secret of this treasure, there will be no genre where he will not attain his goal, though there are some verses which are not suitable for this book. Some are beyond the mind of every one and no one will be able to understand them. Some are outwardly clothed in locks, moles, lips and mouths; their wording is the same as that current among professionals (*ahl-i rasm*?). As they had been composed, however, I entered them together into a single necklace, because looking at a mole without seeing the face, or at a face without seeing the mole, amounts to being shortsighted.*

Anthologies

Quatrains have been composed by innumerable poets, both under their own name and anonymously. To compile an inventory of this huge output one would have to go beyond the *dīvāns* and other collections devoted to a single author, and examine the anthologies of Persian poetry. Throughout the centuries, anthologies have been compiled in various forms.[26] A special category among these works are the *tazkiras* ('Memoirs') which also contain information on the lives of the poets. From this vast literature only one work can be mentioned here: *Riyāẕ al-'ārifīn* ('The Pastures of the Mystics'),[27] compiled in 1844 by Riẕā-Qulī Khān Hidāyat (1800–71), the last great anthologist in the traditional style. This anthology is exclusively devoted to Sufi saints who were also renowned as poets. Designed on more modern lines is Hoceÿne Azad's *Gulzār-i ma'rifat* ('The Rosegarden of understanding'), a collection of 470 mystical quatrains accompanied by French translations.[28]

Other important sources are the mystical prose texts which contain poetical quotations, often in the form of rubā'īyāt. As we have seen already, works like Ibn Munavvar's hagiography and Najm ad-Dīn Dāya's *Mirṣād al-'ibād* provide valuable information on the early stage of the history of the Persian quatrain. A long list of other titles could be added, for example Aḥmad Ghazālī's *Savāniḥ*, a treatise of the theory of love, Maybūdī's mystical commentary on the Koran, and the works of the great mystic 'Ayn al-Quẕāt Hamadānī, who all lived in the first half of the twelfth century.

Commentaries

Most quatrains are simple poems which can easily be interpreted once the poet's point has been understood. Yet, sometimes the meaning of a quatrain was considered to be in need of a commentary. The most remarkable instance is the poem called *Rubā'ī-yi ḥaurā'īya* ('The quatrain of the Heavenly Maidens', i.e. the houris, the women with 'white, big eyes' who, according to the Koran, await the arrival of the blessed in Paradise) after the poem's opening:

The Heavenly Maidens stood in a row to look at my Idol;
The Keeper of Paradise clapsed his hands in admiration;
That black mole on the cheeks was a robe of silk;
For fear the holy men clutched their Korans.

The poem belongs to the corpus of Abū Sa'īd's quatrains. It is mentioned in Ibn Munavvar's *Asrār at-tauḥīd* within the context of an anecdote which tells that the Master, on hearing that his 'reciter' (*muqrī*) Bū Ṣāliḥ had fallen ill, sent him an amulet on which this quatrain was written. It was not uncommon that magical power was ascribed to quatrains as it appears from notes added to some of the collections of Abū Sa'īd's poems. This quatrain, however, is a special case because, during the fourteenth and fifteenth centuries, it roused the interest of several prominent mystics. There are at least twelve short commentaries known, each expounding in its own way the symbolic meanings read into the poem.

The poet Muḥammad Maghribī (d. 1406–07) was the first to identify the Idol of the quatrain with Adam, whom God 'made in His own image' and therefore astounded the spiritual beings with his perfect beauty reflecting the inaccessible Divine Essence. This line of interpretation was further developed by Qāsim-i Anvār (d. 1433–34). The therapeutic force of the poem was, in his view, due to sheikh Abū Sa'īd's becoming the interpreter of the 'Tongue of the Unseen'. Shāh Ni'mat-Allāh Valī (d. 1431), the founder of the great Ni'mat-Allāhī Sufi Order, wrote several essays on this quatrain. The fairly straightforward imagery was burdened with a number of abstract concepts derived from the doctrine of Ibn al-'Arabī on the Unity of Being. Closer to the original meaning remained another great sheikh, 'Ubayd-Allāh Aḥrār (d. 1490), the dominating personality of the Naqshbandī Order in the late fifteenth century. He observed:

The recitation of this quatrain to a sick person indicates that there is something in the rubā'ī which causes lovers to rejoice. This thing is that what reminds the lovers' spirits of that state in which they, with a myriad of perceptions and longings, will return to God.[29]

Mullā 'Abd ar-Raḥmān Jāmī (1414–92), who was also a Naqshbandī sheikh, used quatrains for an exposition of mystical philosophy in a different manner. In his *Sharḥ-i rubā'īyāt* ('Commentary of quatrains'), he explained forty-four poems, all written by him and dealing with 'the Unity of Being and Its modes of descending to the stages where It can be perceived'. This central theme of speculative mysticism returns in many of Jāmī's works. One of the quatrains in this treatise represents the seclusion as well as the exposure of transcendental being in the image of a lady in her boudoir; she is contemplating her beauty in the mirrors of a universe which owes its existence to no one but herself:

There was only the Beloved Woman, looking into
A myriad of mirrors put in front of Her.
Each of these mirrors reflected Her face,
In different grades of clarity and pureness.[30]

Jāmī used the same image in an extended form in the prologue of his allegorical *masnavī* poem *Yūsuf va Zulaykhā*:

In private room where being had no sign,
The world was stored away in non-existence,
One Being was, untouched by duplication,
Far beyond any talk of 'we' and 'you';
A Beauty sat, detached from all appearance,
Visible only to Herself by Her own light;
A ravishing Beloved in seclusion,
Her garment still unsoiled by imperfection.
No mirror held reflections from Her face,
No comb could pass its fingers through Her ringlets.
No wind was able to unbind a single hair.
Her eye had never seen the slightest make-up.
. . .
The love-songs that she heard were all her own;
No lover played with her but She alone.
However, as the beautiful are bound to,
She also could not suffer Her seclusion.
. . .
If this must be, wherever beauty dwells,
Such urge arose first from Eternal Beauty.
She moved Her tent outside the sacred bounds,
Revealed Herself to souls and to horizons.
A different face appeared in every mirror.
Her Being was discussed in every place.[31]

These two quotations show how a single subject could be treated both in the smallest and in the largest form of Sufi poetry, and so they demonstrate the basic unity of the tradition which we will further explore in the following chapters.

Notes

1. Browne, LHP iii, pp. 211–22; Arberry, CPL, pp. 308–16; Rypka, EI, s.v. Ibn-i Yamīn and HIL, p. 261.
2. Cf. L.P. Elwell-Sutton, *The Persian Metres*, pp. 252–56, and the same, 'The "rubā'ī" in early Persian literature', in CHI, 4, pp. 633–57; C.-H. de Fouchécour, EI, s.v. Rubā'ī.

3. The origin of FitzGerald's poem was investigated by A.J. Arberry, *The romance of the Rubaiyat*, London 1959.
4. The article was published in an English translation by E. Denison Ross in *Journal of the Royal Asiatic Society*, Vol. xxx, 1898, pp. 349–66.
5. Among the abundant literature on Khayyām the monograph by Ali Dashti, *In search of Omar Khayyam*, London 1971 (translated and introduced by L.P. Elwell-Sutton) and A.J. Boyle, 'Umar Khayyām: astronomer, mathematician and poet' in CHI, 4, pp. 658–64, are to be recommended. For an up-to-date survey of the question, with a full bibliography, see De Blois, PL, v/2, pp. 356–80.
6. Robert Graves and O. Ali-Shah, *The Rubaiyyat of Omar Khayyam*, London 1967; the hoax of an non-existent manuscript was unmasked by J.C.E. Bowen, *Translation or travesty? An enquiry into Robert Graves's version of some Rubaiyat of Omar Khayyam*, Abingdon 1973.
7. J.B. Nicolas, *Les quatrains de Khèyam*, Paris 1867, p. 8.
8. *Mirṣād al-'ibād*, p. 31; transl. H.Algar, p. 54.
9. *Ilāhī-nāma*, ed. F. Rūḥānī, p. 215; transl. J.A. Boyle, pp. 252–53.
10. V. Minorsky, EI, s.v. Bābā-Ṭāhir.
11. The entire anecdote was translated by E.G. Browne, LHP ii, p. 260, from the Persian chronicle *Rāḥat aṣ-ṣudūr*, written by Muḥammad Rāvandī about 1204.
12. In an Istanbul manuscript, M. Mīnuvī found a few of Bābā Ṭāhir's poems which show the traces of a Western Persian dialect in a more pronounced form than one usually finds; see Z̲. Ṣafā, *Tārīkh-i adabīyāt dar Īrān*, ii, 3rd ed., Tehran 1339 (1960), pp. 384–86.
13. On the *qalandars* and the antinomian motives in Sufi poetry see below, Chapter 3, pp. 71–76.
14. See in particular: Reynold A. Nicholson, 'Abú Sa'íd ibn Abi'l-Khayr' in *Studies in Islamic Mysticism*, Cambridge, 1921, pp. 1–76, and Fritz Meier, *Abū Sa'īd-i Abū l-H̲ayr. Wirklichkeit und Legende*, Leiden, 1976.
15. Ed. Shafī'ī Kadkanī, i, p. 16.
16. Cited by A.J. Arberry, CPL, p. 71.
17. *Sukhanān-i manẓūm*, Nos. 102, 120, 123, 195 and 31.
18. W. Chittick, Enc.Ir., s.v. Bābā Afẓal-al-Dīn.
19. The collection was described by H. Ritter, in Oriens, Vol. 13–14, 1961, pp. 195–228, who earlier translated 'Aṭṭār's introduction into German in *Der Islam*, Vol. 25, 1938, pp. 152–55.
20. *Mukhtār-nāma*, p. 65, Chapter 11 ('On the things one cannot say and know about the hidden world and the spirit'), No. 1.

21. Op.cit., p. 146, Chapter 30 ('On distancing oneself from the beloved'), No. 6.
22. Op.cit., p. 208, Chapter 44 ('Poems on qalandars and wine'), No. 11; about the 'girdle of unbelief', the *zunnār*, see below p. 76.
23. Op.cit., p. 215, Chapter 45 ('On the meanings attached to the rose'), No. 5.
24. Op.cit., p. 222, Chapter 46 ('On the meanings attached to dawn'), No. 14.
25. Op.cit., p. 247, Chapter 49 ('On speaking through the mouth of the moth'), No. 5.
26. On Persian anthologies see EI, s.v. Mukhtārāt. 2.
27. Hidāyat's anthology was first published as a lithograph, Tehran 1305 (1888); cf. Storey, PL, i/2, p. 911.
28. *La roseraie du savoir. Golzâr-é ma'réfèt*, 2 vols., Paris and Leiden 1906.
29. On these commentaries, see Nafīsī, *Sukhanān-i manẓūm*, pp. 125–42; Shafī'ī-Kadkanī, *Asrār at-tauḥīd*, i, muqaddama, pp. 119–27 and text, pp. 274–75 (the anecdote). Shaykh Aḥrār's *Risāla-yi Ḥaurā'īya* was published by V. Zhukovsky at the end of his edition of *Asrār at-tauhīd*, St. Petersburg 1899.
30. *Sharḥ-i rubā'īyāt dar vaḥdat al-vujūd* in *Si risāla dar taṣavvuf*, ed. I. Afshār, Tehran 1360 (1981), p. 85.
31. *Haft Aurang*, pp. 591–92.

2

Poems of Abstinence

The qaṣīda in secular and religious poetry

Up to the end of the eleventh century, the use of quatrains by the Sufis was no more than a marginal phenomenon in Persian literary history. The centres of literary life were not the small communities of mystical sheikhs and their adherents, but the local courts in the eastern parts of the Caliphate, where the Persian language had gained a footing as a vehicle of higher culture. The concerns of the court poets were largely determined by the functions their art performed within this social framework. To the ruler and his courtiers, poetry was a valuable asset for more than one reason.

First, there was the ritual function which the work of the poets had to fulfill. Like the collection of precious objects and the erection of sumptuous buildings, the patronage of poets belonged to the care for royal status. By tradition, formal odes had to be recited at important sessions of the court, like the seasonal festivals or the celebrations of the military exploits of the prince. As far as their contents are concerned, these odes were a kind of laudatory speech the conventions of which were dictated by the requirements of the occasion. The most important part of its pattern was the actual 'panegyric', or *madīḥ*, consisting of a lengthy enumeration of the patron's qualities. It was by no means meant to provide a realistic description of the person being praised. The image presented by the poet, with all the rhetorical skill at his command, had to be an idealised one; its purpose was to show the patron, not as he actually was, but as he should be seen; as the perfect representative of the category to which he belonged – whether he was a ruler, a general, a minister, or a high member of the Islamic clergy. One may very well compare these verbal pictures to state portraits in Western art.

The second advantage of poetry was closely connected to this nature of the courtly panegyric. Successful poems of this kind were of great value as a boost to the patron's prestige. When they were transmitted to other places and admired there, it was not only the reputation of the poet which benefited, but also that of the patron mentioned in the poem. Thirdly, the poet also catered to the entertainments held at court by writing the texts to be performed by minstrels and musicians. As we will see later, this particular aspect of court poetry was to have a considerable impact on the development of the poetry of the Sufis.

Fourthly, but not least, Persian court poetry was equally appreciated because of the moral instruction it provided. It had always been regarded as one of the fundamental tasks of literature, both in prose and in poetry, to convey secular wisdom, referred to as *khirad* or *ḥikmat*. The Zoroastrian books written in the Pahlavi language are full of maxims, most of which lived on in Persian literature of Islamic times. In the early ninth century, Arab poets like Abū'l-'Atāhiya (d. ca 825) and Abū Nuwās (d. ca. 815), later followed by al-Mutanabbī (915–65), had created a new type of poems devoted to thoughts about the uncertainties of earthly life and the necessity to prepare oneself for death and the afterlife. The name which became attached to this genre was *zuhdīyāt*, 'poems of abstinence'.[1] The word *zuhd*, on which this term was based, belongs to the technical vocabulary of Sufism, but it would be an exaggeration to qualify these sombre reflections of court poets as mystical poetry. There can be no doubt, however, that both the Middle Persian wisdom literature and the Arabic poems of abstinence did exert a great influence on Sufi literature.

This brief sketch of the world of poetry as it flourished

especially in Transoxania, Khurasan and the area now called Afghanistan should provide the necessary background to the rise of a diversified religious literature. Its earliest appearance was in the eleventh century, but the full expansion took place only during the subsequent century.

I deliberately use here the qualification 'religious', rather than 'Sufi' or even 'mystical'. Between secular poetry on the one hand, and the poetry which unequivocally must be classified as mystical, a wide area of literary activity has existed which was religiously motivated without being necessarily identified with Sufism. Throughout the centuries, a multitude of poems were written which give expression to Muslim piety of a general kind, to religious morality, to the veneration of the holy men of Islam and, not in the last place, to the allegiance to the Shi'ite Imams and the compassion with their martyrdom. Although this wide range of religious subjects is not at the centre of our attention, it cannot be entirely disregarded because there is indeed a very close relationship with specifically Sufi poetry.

The verse form dealt with in this chapter is the *qaṣīda,*[2] which was borrowed by religiously minded poets from the literature of the courts. A qaṣīda was originally a long poem of praise written in mono-rhyme (according to the pattern: aa, ba, ca, etc.). Its length could vary between twenty to fifty, or even more, lines. This gave enough scope for the elaboration of a laudatory speech and made it also suitable for hymns on the Prophet Muḥammad, the Imams and other holy figures of the Islamic tradition. However, already the Arabic *zuhdīyāt* poems were qaṣīdas of a different type. They were no longer panegyrics but contained a sequence of reflections usually ending in an admonishing note. Such poems could be called 'sermons on rhyme' and one of the terms to denote them was *mavā'iẓ*, which has this very meaning. It would be mistaken to take this qualification as a slight on the poetic value of qaṣīdas of this kind. On the contrary, in the homiletic genre one finds some of the most forceful poetry written either in Arabic or Persian.

In his famous *Qābūs-nāma,* a 'mirror-for-princes' written about 1082, Kay-Kā'ūs discussed the merits of various literary themes.

Stressing the value of honesty in panegyrics, and warning for excess in satire, he also recommended the choice of more lofty themes:

> *Do not fail [to write poems] on abstention (*zuhd*) and unity (*tauḥīd*), if you are able to do so, because you will benefit from this in both worlds.*[3]

The first of these two terms refers to the ascetic poetry, which was a genre in Arabic poetry mentioned above. The second term refers to more religious subject-matter, which included a statement of the fundamental tenets on the oneness of God held by the Muslim community at large. To complete the repertoire of religious themes treated in homiletic qaṣīdas one should add the praise of the Prophet (*na't*) and that of his immediate successors, al-Khulafā' ar-Rāshidūn ('the Rightly Guided Caliphs', i.e. Abū Bakr, 'Umar, 'Uthmān and 'Alī), according to the concensus of Sunnite Islam. To hymns of the latter kind, the term *manāqib* is usually applied.

Specimens of these hallowed themes are rare in Persian poetry up to the end of the eleventh century, but already in the next century they became a very prominent genre. The treatment of this religious themes was not restricted to qaṣīdas. They also provide the conventional material for the introduction of narrative or didactical poems in *masnavīs*, which we will discuss in a later chapter.

Kisā'ī

The question of the origins is, also in this case, surrounded by many uncertainties. For all we know, the use of courtly forms of poetry for religious purposes in Persian literature may have begun already towards the end of the tenth century.

The first poet to be mentioned, but not without considerable caution, is Majd ad-Dīn Abū'l-Ḥasan Kisā'ī.[4] In fact, very little is certain about him beyond the date of his birth, which he mentioned precisely in one of his poems: Wednesday, 26 Shawwāl 341, or 16 March 953. It is very likely that he came from the city of Marv. He must have lived at least until 998, the beginning of the reign of Sultan Maḥmūd of Ghazna, as he praised the latter in another poem. Of his poetry no more than a few fragments have been preserved. This makes it very difficult to say to what extent Kisā'ī was still involved in the life of the courts, the environment where poets normally made their careers in his days. In the early years of the thirteenth century, the anthologist 'Aufī described him as

> *a poet clad in the garment of abstention and wearing the cap of poverty on his head; he had wiped the earth from the surface of his heart with the sleeve of devotion; he had swept away the dust of desire on the field of his breast with the water of his eyes.*[5]

He adds that the main themes of Kisā'ī's poetry were preaching abstention (*zuhd*), dispensing religious advice (*va'ẓ*) and extolling the virtues of the House of the Prophet. As we do not know how much of Kisā'ī's poetry was still accessible to 'Aufī, it is hard to assess the historical value of his flowery statements. On the other hand, this description fits very well that of 'a solitary ascetic', a qualification Bākharzī (d. 1075), an earlier anthologist who wrote in Arabic, gave to a person who may very well be the poet Kisā'ī himself.

Already in the middle of the twelfth century, the Shi'ites claimed Kisā'ī as one of their own. Actually, a part of a hymn on 'Alī ibn Abī Ṭālib has been preserved in which he states:

> *Regard this belief of Guidance as a circle:*
> *The Prophet being its centre, the periphery 'Alī.*

Such an expression of dedication to one of the greatest figures of Islam, held in veneration by all Muslims, is in itself insufficient proof of his Shi'ite sympathies. Nevertheless, the question to which branch of Shi'ism Kisā'ī actually belonged has been much debated by modern scholars. Central to this discussion are the references to Kisā'ī occurring in the work of another religious poet, whose Shi'ite convictions are beyond any doubt.

Nāṣir-i Khusrau

This poet, Nāṣir-i Khusrau (1004–ca. 1072),[6] was also born at Marv, and became a convert to Ismā'īlī Shi'ism shortly before he departed on the journey to Mecca and Egypt, which he described in his famous travelogue *Safar-nāma*. In the eleventh century, Cairo was not only the capital of the Fatimid Caliphate was, but at the same time the ideological centre of the Ismā'īlī movement. In Cairo, Nāṣir studied at the learned institutions of his newly adopted creed, where he was trained to serve as a missionary in his homeland. After his return, he spent the rest of his life more or less as a fugitive in Badakhshan, a mountainous area in the north-east of present-day Afghanistan. He wrote several philosophical treatises attempting to demonstrate the congruence of Hellenistic wisdom and learning with the teachings of the Koran, which was a fundamental tenet of the Ismā'īlīya. He also abundantly used the qaṣīda as a medium for his religious teaching. In several of these poems, he made the claim that he excelled Kisā'ī as a religious poet.[7]

It seems incongruous to find such petty rivalry with a predecessor in the poetry of a man so much devoted to religious ideals. Some commentators have seen this as a part of a sectarian quarrel between representatives of different branches of Shi'ism. However, it can perhaps be better explained as a relic of Nāṣir's own past. As he tells in one of his poems, prior to his conversion, he was a clerk (*dabīr*) in the bureaucracy of the Ghaznavid state and also practised profane poetry. The condemnation of these wordly occupations occurs time and again in his qaṣīdas. Though they are didactical in tone and contents, they often end in the praise of the Fatimid Caliph al-Mustanṣir (1036–94) who was not only the living Imam of the Ismā'īlites but also a secular ruler.

It is difficult to gauge Nāṣir-i Khusrau's influence on the development of Persian mystical poetry. In his time, Ismā'īlism was a religious movement with strong political aspirations. It had little in common with the circles of the Sufis, who kept themselves remote from the world cultivating their inner souls and striving after a personal, rather than a collective conformity to the will of God. These Sufis were, moreover, nearly all devout Sunnites, and were rarely interested in questions of dogma or in the political problems of the Muslim community.

On the other hand, Nāṣir-i Khusrau's importance as the creator of new forms of religious poetry cannot be overlooked. His odes are full of the same homiletic themes and motifs in which the works of later Sufi poets abound. In the hands of Nāṣir-i Khusrau, the Persian qaṣīda was turned into an effective tool for religious and ethical instruction. Another interesting feature of his didacticism is its close link to metaphysics. The spiritual development of the human being amounted, in the view of the Ismā'īlīya, to a gnostic search of the universe, which was the only way towards an escape from its bondage in the material world. As we will see, the prominent role assigned to knowledge about the structure of the world was equally important to the Sufi poets. Finally, it cannot be denied that in the adaptation of forms of secular poetry the work of Nāṣir-i Khusrau provides us with the first instance of a process which proved to be of great importance to our subject.

Sanā'ī

In view of the isolation in which Nāṣir-i Khusrau lived it is difficult to imagine how his works could have made an impact outside the social circles of the Ismā'īlīya which, being a persecuted heterodox minority, had little contact with the Sunnite Muslim community. This question is, for lack of evidence, unanswerable. It cannot be denied, however, that Nāṣir's religious qaṣīdas show many similarities to those of Majdūd ibn Ādam Sanā'ī, who was born at Ghazna in the late eleventh century and died in that city in 1131. It is generally acknowledged that Sanā'ī was one of the founders of Persian Sufi poetry.

Fortunately, he left an extensive *oeuvre* which, in his case, makes it possible to substantiate this reputation. Moreover, several ancient manuscripts of his works have survived, some of which can be dated as early as the twelfth century and therefore constitute philological material of great value for the study of his contribution to the tradition.

His collected works also provide us with the material for an outline of his biography. In fact, his life is far better known than that of most Persian poets of the Middle Ages. This is a very fortunate circumstance, because it makes it possible to trace his personal development, which is exemplary for the development of Sufi poetry itself at this early stage. Towards the end of the eleventh century, Sanā'ī tried to become a court poet at Ghazna, the residence of the Ghaznavid Sultans who earlier in the same century had been lavish patrons of Persian poetry. As it seems, he was not very successful, however, in realising this ambition. He did find an entrance to circles close to the court, but was never personally patronised by Mas'ūd III, the Sultan of those days. On the other hand, it is remarkable that several of his early poems are in praise of prominent Islamic scholars in Ghazna. These contacts will have been helpful in determining the further course of his career.

In the early years of the twelfth century, Sanā'ī left Ghazna and went to Khurasan, which was then outside the territories governed by the Ghaznavids. In this new environment, he abandoned the search for patrons among the political elite. Instead, he wandered from one city to another establishing contacts with men who belonged exclusively to the religious classes. They were either members of the Muslim clergy or Sufis. The former category seems to have been the most important to him. It included judges, theologians and preachers who often were very influential personalities locally. By far the most important among these patrons was Sayf ad-Dīn Muḥammad ibn Manṣūr, a religious scholar following the school of Abū Ḥanīfa and the Chief Justice of the city of Sarakhs. In several poems, Sanā'ī gave expression to his deep gratitude towards this patron, who apparently helped him to lay the practical foundation for his religious poetry.

There is a curious mixture of worldly and spiritual interests to be noted in the panegyrics that Sanā'ī wrote for this clerical patron. On the one hand, Muḥammad ibn Manṣūr acted like any other social protector by providing Sanā'ī with the material support he needed. On the other hand, the relationship between patron and client quite clearly also included a spiritual bond. The Chief Justice was renowned as a great preacher, who had built his own convent (*khānaqāh*) at Sarakhs to serve as the place where his flock gathered. Sanā'ī's religious poems must have been most welcome to him as they clothed the preacher's sermons in a poetic form.

As far as the Sufis are concerned, there is evidence of Sanā'ī's visit to a mystical community at Herat which was led by descendants of 'Abd-Allāh Anṣārī, one of the great Sufi sheikhs of the eleventh century. An exchange of poems with one of the mystics of Herat has been preserved. It seems, however, that the relationship with the preacher-judge of Sarakhs was the decisive factor to Sanā'ī's career during the years of his stay in Khurasan. It is, therefore, appropriate to characterise him, from this turning-point onwards, as a 'homiletic' poet. This qualification is more apt than that of a 'Sufi' poet, because the former term defines more precisely the environment where his poems originated as well as the purpose they primarily had to serve. The same term still applies to the last phase of his career, when he began his final great work, the *Fakhrī-nāma,* or *Ḥadīqat al-ḥaqīqa*. This extensive didactical poem (to which I will return later) was not intended, in the first place, for a Sufi audience, but for Bahrāmshāh, the Sultan residing in Ghazna when Sanā'ī had returned there towards the end of his life.

Labelling Sanā'ī's work as essentially homiletic – that is: written to serve the preaching of Muslim piety in a general sense – does in no way diminish the great importance of this *oeuvre* to the further development of Sufi poetry. Sanā'ī's various forms of religious poetry, his use of imagery and the themes he treated of, made a great impact on later Sufi poets and writers. The growing interest in mysticism that can be witnessed in the eleventh and twelfth centuries throughout the Persian-speaking area created the need for a new idiom for the expression of spiritual ideas beyond the technical language of Sufism which had been created already by theoretical writers. Sanā'ī appeared on the scene just at the right moment and this explains the remarkable impact made by his poems. It is also evident that Sanā'ī's reputation was established very soon, perhaps during in his own lifetime. Lines from his poems were cited already by several writers who were his contemporaries.

The influence of Sanā'ī's innovations makes it necessary to devote to him several pages of the present survey, not only in this chapter but also in the following chapters on the *ghazal*s and the *masnavī*s. For now, we will only discuss some of his homiletic poems which were written as qaṣīdas.

Sanā'ī's zuhdīyāt

In the qaṣīdas assembled in some of the early Sanā'ī-manuscripts under the heading *zuhdīyāt*, we find the entire range of religious subjects represented. These poems not only exhibit a varied content, they are also of quite different lengths. The longest is a qaṣīda of about 140 distichs with the sumptuous Arabic title *Kunūz al-ḥikma va rumūz al-mutaṣavvifa* ('The treasures of wisdom and the symbols of Sufism').[8] It is very unlikely that Sanā'ī himself gave this name to the poem, but its presence in many manuscripts of his *Dīvān* is a sure sign of the prominence of this qaṣīda among his *zuhdīyāt* poems.

The early popularity of the poem is attested by a quotation in the Persian adaptation of the Indian book of fables *Kalīla va Dimna* made by Naṣr-Allāh Munshī, a secretary in the service of the Ghaznavid sultans, who dedicated his work to Sultan Bahrāmshāh about 1145, that is only a few years after the death of Sanā'ī:

There is a Witness in the world, but we are idle;
There is a draught left in the cup, but we remain sober.
Arise! Let us set to rest, with the water from our faces,

The wind blowing from this deceitful heap of earth.
Let's sally forth on a raid and let's destroy
The marketplace where this blackfaced soul thrives![9]

This instance of borrowing is an illuminating one, as it shows how freely the poet's contemporaries availed themselves of Sanā'ī's work, divorcing passages not only from their context but also from their original meaning. To the writer of a mirror-for-princes like the *Kalīla va Dimna* these lines were no more then the apt phrasing of a hedonistic escapism. The quotation is made in the context of a story about real pleasures: a tired king, who wishes to withdraw for a while from the world, seeks the comfort of his private circle.

Sanā'ī's intention was certainly quite different. In the poem the same lines serve him as the beginning of a stern homily. The anacreontic motives, like the 'witness' (in Persian *shāhid*, the representative of supernatural beauty in the flesh) and the draught of wine, symbolise a detachment from the world of a much more radical kind. This even includes the abandoning of such sacred values as worshipping the Ka'ba, by which Sanā'ī aims at an easy form of piety indulged in by those who shrink from the 'intoxication' of an absolute commitment to the Eternal.

The first part of the sermon elaborates the theme of the struggle with the 'black-faced soul' by showing the pernicious influence of the powers of this world, that is the heavenly bodies and the natural elements held responsible for the wicked inclinations of the soul. In order to escape from this existential bondage, one should renounce 'existence' (*būd*), meaning all that by which one is attached to this world:

The heart (dil) *is a village* (dih) *when it is filled*
With cattle, donkeys, goods and chattels.

Sanā'ī's discourse abounds in such homely examples which, as in the present example, are often enforced by wordplay. They alternate freely with expressions of more profound ideas, for instance in the following lines where the contrast is used between the negative and the positive statements in the first half of the declaration of faith, the *shahāda*, 'There no god other than God':

In the gallery of God's Command no statues
Of believers or unbelievers can be seen:
Deep in the ocean of 'Other than God' lives
The snake 'No' who devours belief and unbelief.

To understand the full force of this conceit one should know that the Arabic word *lā* ('no') resembles in writing the wide-open jaws of a monster. Again, the poet's words should be listened to with due regard to his intention. As he makes perfectly clear in the course of this long poem, the irrelevance of belief and unbelief to the fulfilment of God's will is not to be equated with an antinomian attitude. To the contrary, the way he shows consists of a submission to the law of Islam, the light which has the power to conquer the darkness of 'existence'. He leaves no doubt about this in the following passage:

No better leaders guiding you on the Path of God
Than the Koran and the sacred Traditions.
Only Muḥammad's hand and heart are able
To take care of the secrets' treasury (the human heart).
If your heart is filled by Aḥmad's light,
Be assured that you are saved from the Fire.

In spite of this emphasis on a strict obedience to God's commands, Sanā'ī's message also contains a strongly emotional appeal which shows the mystical foundation of his Islamic orthodoxy. The Anacreontic prelude, with its apparent antinomian note, is echoed by words on the significance of love as the moving force which only can bring man nearer to God:

Reason cannot go along the path of Love;
Do not expect to see with those blind eyes.
In Love's domain the Intellects lack power,
Whatever they pretend with their idle doings.

Another poem which attracted the attention of Sanā'ī's contemporaries was the qaṣīda opening with the exhortation:

Do not make the body and the soul your dwelling place:
the first one is inferior, the second is superior.
Go outside these two [stages]; do not stay on neither here nor there.[10]

In this poem Sanā'ī sets out to admonish his audience about the necessity for the human being to transcend the limitations set by his worldly existence. A concatenation of themes, which are recurrently broached in the *zuhdīyāt*, is used to bring this warning home: one should seek a death while still in this world by letting oneself be killed by words of love so that eternal life may be found; one should not trust the world because, by her very unfaithfulness (*bad-mihrī*), she warns you not to rely on her; one should be aware of the dangers of false piety and not boast of one's knowledge of the laws of Islam or one's asceticism ('the [empty] air of jurisprudence, the [empty] air of poverty'); one should take part in a spiritual war against the tyranny of the body; wisdom and knowledge must never be sought out of greed. The last mentioned piece of advice is illustrated by a line which lives on in the Persian language as a proverbial warning against an intellectualism which is not held in check by morality:

If you have acquired knowledge out of greed,
be careful, for in the night
A thief makes a better choice from your goods
when he carries a lamp.

The poem as a whole provides a remarkable instance of the pointed formulation of homiletic wisdom which was the hallmark of Sanā'ī's style. The wide reception of the poem can be demonstrated by listing the mystical writers who cited one or more of its lines: in the twelfth century, we find citations in the letters of 'Ayn al-Quẓāt Hamadānī (executed in 1131, the year of Sanā'ī's own death), in the Sufi commentary on the Koran by Rashīd ad-Dīn Maybūdī (begun in 1126), in the writings of the gnostic philosopher Shihāb ad-Dīn Yaḥyā Suhravardī (in 1191 executed at Aleppo as a heretic) and the Shirazi mystic Rūzbihān-i Baqlī (1128–1209); in the following century, the same poem was cited from by the historian Rāvandī (who wrote ca. 1204) and the mystics Najm ad-Dīn Dāya (d. 1256), Shams-i Tabrīzī and Sulṭān Valad, the latter two belonging to the entourage of Maulānā Jalāl al-Dīn Rūmī.

Some of Sanā'ī's longer poems are distinguished by the use of extended allegories. In one instance, he gave an account of a pilgrimage to Mecca which looks like a poetic travelogue, but is in fact merely a device to illustrate the self-sacrifice demanded of the follower of God's commands. In the first section of the poem Sanā'ī traces the itinerary of an actual pilgrimage, including a visit to the grave of the Imam Abū Ḥanīfa in Iraq, incumbent upon a follower of the Ḥanafī school of Islamic law. Then the account takes a surprising turn: having sketched how intensely the exhausted pilgrim looks forward to his destination, the poet all of a sudden brings up the suggestion that this pilgrim could die before he reached his goal. If he were truly a traveller to God, he would even accept this final ordeal:

Each arrow hitting us from God's battlefield we will make
Into a gift to the soul; we ourselves will be the arrow's point.[11]

A very daring kind of symbolisation is to be found in a poem he wrote for the Chief Justice of Sarakhs, Muḥammad ibn Manṣūr. He availed himself of the fortuitous circumstance that the latter's name was also the name of the Prophet. Although the poem, in the end, proves to be a panegyric to a real patron, the first half of the text consists of a curious interpretation of one of the shorter chapters of the Koran, Sūra xciii. The oath contained in the first verse of this Sūra ('By the white forenoon and the brooding night!') is taken to refer symbolically to the twofold nature of the Prophet's personality in which the lightness of religion and the darkness of the world that he had to live in were combined. This ambiguity corresponded externally to the shining face and the dark locks – a motif taken again from the imagery of erotic poetry.

To make his turn towards the praise of his patron, Sanā'ī resorts to the final words of the Sūra: 'And as for thy Lord's blessing, declare it!.' The analogy of this injunction to make God's bounty known to the Arabs is, as Sanā'ī argues, the obligation incumbent on his own tongue to praise Muḥammad ibn Manṣūr among the Persians.[12]

No more than these few instances of Sanā'ī's homiletic poems can be mentioned here. His *zuhdīyāt* constitute a rich and still largely unexplored mine of imagery standing almost at the beginning of the full development of Persian mystical poetry.

Khāqānī and other twelfth century poets of the qaṣīda

In the history of Persian poetry, the twelfth century is a period of conflicting tendencies. On the one hand, there was a rapid development of forms like the *ghazal* and the *ma̱snavī* which, though not unknown to earlier poets, now assumed a greater and different importance. To some extent this trend can be linked to the expansion of religious poetry which created a demand for a greater variety of forms. On the other hand, the qaṣīda did not yet cede its prominent place in literature, as it was to do in the subsequent centuries. To the contrary, some of the most powerful writers of qaṣīdas of the entire Persian tradition lived in this century. They even added new features to this ancient form, which strengthened its suitability to embody a sustained and rhetorically effective discourse. One of these changes was the increased use of Arabic vocabulary, a trend which was closely related to the extension of the imagery of poetry to include many items derived from the sciences and the other arts. These poets represented the type of the *poeta doctus*, to whom the pursuit of learning had opened a rich source of comparisons and metaphors. This does not mean, however, that these poets were great scholars, as it has been often assumed by traditional biographers. It is more accurate to say that they were people with a general education who used the bits of learning they had acquired to their own ends, which were not scholarly but literary.

Another characteristic of this period is that the reinforced qaṣīda was employed in court poetry as well as in poetry of a religious nature. Actually, it proves to be difficult to make a proper distinction between the two spheres. One of the great masters of the qaṣīda in this new style, Anvarī,[13] who lived in Khurasan and whose date of death in the second half of the century remains unestablished, was in every respect a poet of the court. Apart from occasional complaints about the negative aspects of his profession and some didactic passages praising the virtue of contentment (*qanā'at*), there are no traces of Sufism in his works.

Much more complex is the picture presented by the life of Anvarī's counterpart in Western Persia, Afẕal ad-Dīn Ibrahīm Khāqānī (ca. 1126–99).[14] He was during most of his career a court poet dependent on the patronage of the local rulers of his native Sharvān. He also praised a great many other people who not only belonged to the secular elite but also to the Islamic clergy. Late in his life he retreated from the world to a solitary existence in the city of Tabriz. The signs of his inclination towards ascetism and Islamic piety are, however, pervasive in his works. Several of his great qaṣīdas are purely religious poems which contain only praise of God, His Prophet or the Ka'ba in Mecca as the sacred symbol of Islam. On the other hand, there are no indications to be found of a special affiliation with a Sufi master or an attachment to any Sufi milieu. In this respect, Khāqānī's position is not unlike that of Sanā'ī and this is not the only similarity between the two poets. He made no secret of his admiration for the 'wise man' (*ḥakīm*) of Ghazna and boasted that he had come to 'replace' him in the world.

Nevertheless, it would be mistaken to regard Khāqānī as a mere imitator of Sanā'ī. Even more than Anvarī, he created his own extremely sophisticated style. Apart from the features mentioned above, it is marked by an almost inexhaustible inventiveness of original poetic motifs, called *ma'ānī* ('concetti', according to a term current in Western literary criticism), which were elaborated with the application of intricated rhetorical figures. Although a similar style can be noticed with other poets of this period, in particular with the epic poet Niẓāmī of Ganja, Khāqānī's handling of this idiom has remained unequalled in the history of Persian poetry.

The themes broached by Khāqānī in his religious poetry are mostly limited to the sphere of the *zuhdīyāt*, which was defined earlier in this chapter. He condemns the world and preaches the necessity to withdraw from it into a life of poverty and contentment; he denounces the tyranny of the lower soul pointing the way towards inner purification which is also the path to a deliverance from the world and a preparation for the life to come. The note of a complaint is frequently struck in his poems, not only with regard to his spiritual distress, but also in matters of a more mundane nature, such as his dealings with his patrons. In some poems he describes his situation as an 'emprisonment', but it is doubtful whether this should be taken as a reference to a real captivity.[15] The veneration of the Prophet is a recurrent theme, often combined with descriptions of the pilgrimage, the Ka'ba and the Prophet's grave in Medina. To his favourite images belong emblems of light and rebirth like the sun, fire, the rise of dawn and the awakening of nature in spring.

One of Khāqānī's most impressive poems is a long qaṣīda to which the Arabic title *Mir'āt aṣ-ṣafā* ('The Mirror of Purity') has become attached.[16] It is a perfect example of a homiletic poem developing a string of themes with a discursive coherence revealing itself if one carefully traces its line of thought through the seemingly random use of images and rhetorical conceits. The qaṣīda tells of the poet's dealings with his own heart, which in the course of the poem is identified as his *himmat*, a term which R.A. Nicholson has translated by 'holy aspiration'.[17] At first he represents the heart as a teacher from whom he learns how to kill the lower soul and bury it in a 'grave' where it will be guarded by Islamic Law. Then he switches to another metaphor: a king invites the poet to his table and speaks to him about poverty and withdrawal from the world, the ideals of a derwish's life. This is how, at the beginning of this discourse, he draws the picture of a Koranic school as an extended metaphor of his meditation:

heart is a sheikh who teaches me,
the child who understands his language.
w my head I pay him my fee,
wnen I put my head on my knees I attend his school.
Not on every knee his school can be found;
Not all moments are tablets to receive his words.
Not every sea hides shells,
Not every drop is an April shower.
Kneeling down is only a school,
Like Noah's Ark, to him
Whose sorrow is a frothing Flood,
To whom Ararat is a haven.
However, to him who, once,
Enters this school by kneeling down,
The Ararat will not be higher than his ankle-bone,
The Flood will not reach his shank.
No one qualifies for this school
Unless he has a sorrow so great that,
With each breath he inhales, four Floods
Invade the four elements of his body.
The school of kneeling down is meant
Especially for those men who, being lions,
Like a dog shy away behind a knee
From all the agitation among men.

The first step to take, according to the heart's teaching, is to silence the voice of the eager soul and to return to a state of spiritual simplicity:

All heart's lessons are sacred signs,
Which can only be explained by silence.
All he teaches are problems
To be solved by nothing but ignorance.
First he wrote down for me the a-b-c
On the tablet of silence,
For speaking is a headache
To be cured only by silence.

He began by taking away my tongue,
Because a child in his first lessons
Should be without a tongue like the flute,
Not one who knows how to speak like the lute.

The impact of Sanā'ī's homiletic style, so brilliantly exemplified in Khāqānī's poetry, extended to many other poets of the twelfth century. Worth mentioning is Qivāmī,[18] a little known poet from Rayy, near modern Tehran, because he was an avowed Shi'ite. Like Khāqānī he prided himself in being 'another Sanā'ī' and called the latter 'the master of the poets' (*khvāja-yi shā'irān*). Two poets of Isfahan, Jamāl ad-Dīn Muḥammad ibn 'Abd ar-Razzāq (d. 1192)[19] and his son Kamāl ad-Dīn Ismā'īl (ca. 1172–1237),[20] were also notable followers of Sanā'ī's. Their position with regard to the literature of the 'world' was comparable to that of Khāqānī. The expression they gave to the ideals of renunciation and an ascetic way of life contrasts with their quite evident role as panegyrists, even if their main patrons were prominent scholars in Isfahan who were in control of the politics of that city. Modern critics have condemned them for this (A.J. Arberry even called Ismā'īl 'a bogus anchorite'[21]), but indictments of this kind only beg the question of the symbiosis of religious and courtly poetry, one of the most intriguing problems presented by medieval Persian literature.

The qaṣīdas of 'Aṭṭār

There is no question about Farīd ad-Dīn 'Aṭṭār's position within the tradition of Sufi poetry, as we saw already in the previous chapter where his collection of mystical quatrians was discussed. Although the emphasis of his work was on other forms, especially the *ghazal* and the *masnavī*, 'Aṭṭār also left a number of homiletic qaṣīdas. They are quite interesting specimens of the genre which deserve a more detailed examination than it is possible to enter upon here. However, one feature should be mentioned as it adds significantly to the characteristics of *zuhdīyāt* poetry noted already, namely the use of narratives. The first poem in the collection, as it occurs in the edition of the *Dīvān*,[22] includes samples of several topics current in this genre. The themes of God's Unity (*tauḥīd*), the praise of the Prophet (*na't*) and the Heavenly Journey (*mi'rāj*) are all included, serving to build up an impressive homily on the subject of man's insignificance when faced with the radiance of the Divine. In addition to a varied imagery, 'Aṭṭār also inserts a fable:

A gnat, so it is told, was sitting at the seaside,
Bowing its head in deep thought, deploring its weakness.
When asked what it wanted so badly, the poor gnat replied:
'I wished I could hold all this water!', it said.
'You could not contain it, they said, don't say such things!'
It answered: 'But how could I consent to despair?
Do not regard the impotence of my body;
Look from where the desire to attain this arose!'.

To conclude this brief survey, a few words need to be said about the qaṣīda as it was used by later poets. It could be argued with some justification that the rise of the religious qaṣīda since the time of Sanā'ī saved the form from complete oblivion. After the twelfth century, its role as a medium of court poetry was sharply diminished and it remained very much in the background until the neo-classicist revival of the Qajar period. Instead the qaṣīda became primarily a vehicle of religious praise directed towards the Prophet and, increasingly, also to the Imam 'Alī and his descendants. A growing interest in the writing of this kind of poems, designated as *manāqib* ('[enumeration] of virtues') can be noticed already before the general spread of Shi'ite Islam in Persia under the Safavids. The central theme of these poems was, quite naturally, the lament for the suffering of the holy martyrs at the battle of Kerbela (680) where the third Imam Ḥusayn and his followers were slaughtered by their Ummayad foes. Most *manāqibs* were, therefore, elegies which gained great popularity because of their usefulness for the religious ceremonies during the festival of Muḥarram. The most famous poem of this kind was the *duvāzdah-band* by the Safavid poet Muḥtasham (d. 1587).[23] This poem was not written as a qaṣīda, but in the more elaborate form of a stanzaic poem, consisting of a sequence of short stanzas with different rhymes linked together only by their final lines. Several variations of these forms have been created but their importance to our subject is only slight.

Notes

1. Cf. E. Wagner, *Grundzüge der klassischen arabischen Dichtung*, ii, Darmstadt 1988, pp. 120–30.
2. See Stefan Sperl and Christopher Shackle, *Qasida Poetry in Islamic Asia and Africa*, 2 vols., Leiden 1996, especially the contributions by Julie Scott Meisami and Michael Glünz on Persian qaṣīdas, Vol. i, pp. 137–203.
3. *Qābūs-nāma*, p. 191.
4. EI, s.v. Kisā'ī, and De Blois, PL, v/1, pp. 179–80 with further bibliographical references.
5. Muḥammad 'Aufī, *Lubāb al-albāb*, Part ii, ed. by E.G. Browne, London-Leiden 1903, p. 33.
6. The edition of his *Dīvān-i ash'ār*, by N. Taqavī contains a still valuable essay on his life and poetry by Ḥasan Taqīzāda; see further De Blois, PL, v/1, pp. 201–06.
7. See the examples translated by Browne, LHP, ii, p. 162.
8. Sanā'ī, *Dīvān*, qaṣīda no. 114.
9. *Tarjama-yi Kalīla va Dimna*, ed. by M. Mīnuvī, Tehran 1343/1964, p. 396 = Sanā'ī, *Dīvān*, p. 396, bb. 4–6.
10. Op.cit., p. 51, qaṣīda No. 19.
11. Op.cit., p. 414, qaṣīda No. 195.
12. This qaṣīda was analysed by A. Schimmel, *And Muhammad is His Messenger*, pp. 195–200. The Koran is quoted, here and elsewhere in this book, from the translation by A.J. Arberry.
13. See Enc.Ir., s.v. Anṣārī.
14. On the life of this poet see B. Reinert, EI s.v. Khākānī.
15. These poems belong to the genre of prison-poetry the most important specimens of which are to be found in the poetry of Mas'ūd-i Sa'd-i Salmān; see EI Suppl., s.v. *Ḥabsiyya*.
16. Khāqānī, *Dīvān*, pp. 209–15.
17. *The Kashf al Maḥjúb*, p. 155; the virtue of *himmat* in the conception of Khāqānī is discussed by A.L.F.A. Beelaert, *A Cure for the Grieving*, privately published, Leiden 1996, pp. 108 ff.

18. De Bruijn, *Of Piety and Poetry*, pp. 12, 253.
19. Rypka, HIL pp. 213–14.
20. Browne, LHP, ii, pp. 540–42; Arberry, CPL, pp. 244–48; Rypka, HIL, p. 214; A.H. Zarrinkoob, EI, s.v. Kamāl al-Dīn.
21. Arberry, CPL, p. 248.
22. 'Aṭṭār, *Dīvān*, pp. 645–49.
23. See EI, s.v. Muḥtas͟ham.

3

Poetry of Love

The theme of love

Love is probably the most universal symbol for the relationship between the mystic and the Divine goal of his quest. Mystics in all cultures have adopted it as an essential part of the verbal means they use to express their desires and their experiences. In the language of love the most elevated thoughts about the relationship between man and his Creator can be put into words, in the most complete manner in which human speech is able to express that mystery for which there are no words. This unique quality of the theme of love derives from its very nature, namely the fact that it is directly concerned with one of the most fundamental experiences of the human soul. As a phenomenon the concept of love cannot be understood without reference to its human and even biological origin. Erotic motives, even in their most abstract usage (for instance in the terminology of Platonic philosophy), are essentially metaphorical. They were derived ultimately from the emotions experienced in the human psyche in the situation of its earthly existence. The derivation is not only a matter of form. The emotions themselves are, in some way or the other, involved in this transformation by which the basically earthly emotion is 'sublimated' (to borrow a term from modern psychology) into a higher state of the spirit. The awareness of this connection between profane and mystical love rests not only on the analysis of a modern observer: it was already quite openly expressed by medieval Persian writers who were knowledgeable about this process of sublimation by their own experience.

'Desire is the mount of the believer.' Taking his cue from this saying, cited on the authority of the Prophet Muḥammad, Ibn 'Abbādī (1097–1152) described the function of this psychological medium in an exposition of the Sufi path. If he went on foot, the seeker would soon be exhausted and loose the force to proceed. Therefore he needs a swift horse in order to persevere until he reaches his goal:

> *Desire is the quality of longing and affliction in the heart, which is activated by the representation of the beauty of its goal. This creates an inner movement and an emotion in the heart inviting it to go on until the goal will be attained. The wish for the beloved sets the heart into motion and makes it desirous. That desire attracting the heart carries on the body and helps the seeker to set out on his way till he sees that there is a better stage than the one he aspires to. Then he will see how he should move to reach that higher stage and orbit.*[1]

Love, consequently, should be defined as an essentially independent force. It cannot be limited by conditions prevailing in the domain where it happens to manifest itself. According to Aḥmad Ghazālī, a contemporary of Ibn 'Abbādī and like him a great mystical preacher,

> *the distinctive orientations of love are incidental. By its essence, it transcends all directions because it needs not turn into any direction in order to be love. However, one never can tell to which land the water will be led by the hand of emotional experience. When a groom mounts the Sultan's horse he does not make it his property, but in itself there is no harm to this.*

Ghazālī illustrates the educational value, which love in its different manifestations might possess, with the help of the parable of a jeweller's training:

> *Sometimes a potsherd or a bead is given into the hands of an apprentice so that he may become a master; sometimes a precious, shining pearl is entrusted to his inexperienced hands, such a pearl as the expert hands of the master would not dare to touch or pierce.*[2]

In the present chapter we will survey the role which love played in Persian mystical poetry. There can be no doubt that this theme belongs to the very core of our subject. Without a proper understanding of the poetry of love, the essentials of this kind of literature will remain a closed book. It is not only extremely rich by itself, it has also been a magnetic kernel to which several other thematical complexes, not immediately concerned with the erotic, became attracted. The historical link with profane poetry constitutes, also in this case, more than a mere external relationship; it is an intrinsic one in the sense mentioned in the preceding paragraphs.

The theme of love is so pervasive that it touches all other forms of mystical poetry. One cannot study the quatrain, the panegyrical ode or the epic genre without being confronted with specimens of love poetry. However, no form of poetry is as closely tied to the theme of love, with all its ramifications, as the Persian *ghazal*.

The ghazal as a prosodic form and as a genre

The form of the classical ghazal can be defined, first, by the formula of its rhyme, secondly by the length of the poem and finally by its subject-matter. The two external features can best be explained with reference to a *qaṣīda*: the pattern of rhyme is the same, but ghazals are much shorter poems; a length of seven distichs has been mentioned as an ideal size though many ghazals have more lines, even up to twice that number.

Two further characteristics of form should be added to this. Often a so-called *radīf* rhyme has been used in ghazals, that is an addition to the rhyme which usually consists of a verb or a noun, but may also vary from a mere suffix to a short phrase. The essential point is that the *radīf* should constitute a morpheme, a linguistic form with a distinct meaning. In many poems the repetition at the end of each rhyming half-verse provides a semantic coherence to the poem in spite of the kaleidoscopic variety of the imagery.[3]

Another feature, which soon became characteristic of ghazals, is the mention of the poet's name in one of the last lines. Only rarely was the poet's personal name used. Instead, a pen name, called *takhalluṣ*, under which Persian poets used to present themselves as artists, was employed. The purport of such conclusions is to suggest that the lyrical statements made in the poem are the expression of emotions experienced by the poet himself. However, one should be careful not to interpret this in a too modern, romantic way. A 'personalisation' of this kind does not make the poem into a personal confession; it is no more than a literary device, belonging to the ghazal as a genre and providing it with a conventional conclusion, which A.J. Arberry appropriately has called a 'clasp theme'.[4]

The subject-matter of the ghazal cannot be described in as few words. In a very general way one could say that a ghazal is a poem of love, using various Anacreontic themes. However, a more detailed examination of its rich contents is required before a satisfactory answer could be given to the question what Persian ghazals are really about.

The ghazal in the history of literature

Before we enter into this, something should be said on the origins and the history of the ghazal. The term itself can be met with from the earliest times in Arabic poetry. In pre-Islamic bedouin poetry, love songs were named so but it is not quite certain that the word was used already to denote separate poems. Perhaps ghazal was originally the name of a particular lyrical topic rather than of a concrete form of poetry. Although a certain amount of influence from Arabic love poetry is undeniable, the origin of the Persian ghazal cannot be seen as a simple continuation of an

Arabic tradition. Oral poetry as it was practised in Persia prior to Islam must have been influential as well; this kind of poetry continued to be the main genre of the repertoire of minstrels during the early Islamic period.

The practice of love poetry in Persian in the tenth and eleventh centuries was initially purely secular. It seems that, during that period, ghazals were still mainly known as songs performed by minstrels. Though most poets of the time must have composed ghazals, hardly any specimen of an independent poem of this kind has survived. One of the reasons for this poor state of documentation may be that these love poems were not considered to be serious enough to be preserved in writing. The only material from which we can form a picture of this early Persian love poetry are the introductive sections of panegyrical *qaṣīdas*, which seem to reflect the love poetry as it was practised at the courts of the Samanid emirs and the early Ghaznavid sultans.

The written ghazals date, as far as we know, from the early twelfth century, when for the first time sizeable collections of them are known to have existed from the *dīvāns* of Persian poets. It may not be accidental that this coincides with the ever more frequent use of ghazals for the expression of mystical love. Ghazals were only considered worthy to be kept for later use and to be distributed to new audiences when they were no longer seen as mere frivolous songs about love and wine.

Since then, the fusion between the secular and the mystical in Persian ghazals has become such an essential characteristic that, in most instances, it is extremely difficult to make a proper distinction between the two. The decision whether a given poem should be called a Sufi ghazal or a profane love song very often does not depend so much on the poem itself, but on what we know about its writer, that is the answer to the question: does the life of the poet provide us with clues of a mystical affiliation, or is the poet only known as a court poet?

There are at least three reasons why one should be very cautious with such deductions. First, the history of Persian literature is still full of uncertainties. Especially in the case of the medieval poets, the evidence available for their biography is usually very slight. Even if we do have traditional accounts of their lives, the distinction between pious fiction and historical reality is often hard to make. Secondly, it should be realised that ghazals were only transmitted as isolated pieces of poetry, detached from the context to which they belonged originally. It may very well be that many poems of a seemingly profane content were actually meant to be used in a Sufi gathering or in a pious sermon where the occasion provided the proper meaning to poems which, taken at face value, might look quite frivolous. Thirdly, it should be considered that the ambiguity of their ultimate meaning has become an essential feature of the genre.

To some extent the interpretative dilemmas just mentioned present themselves in the case of Sanā'ī of Ghazna (d. 1131). There is enough historical evidence to qualify Sanā'ī as a religious poet who was associated with preachers and mystics. He was also the earliest writer of mystical ghazals to leave a substantial collection. We find among them most of the themes and images which secular and mystical poets used alike, and which constituted the common stock drawn upon by all subsequent writers of ghazals. Many of these poems would not be classified as mystical poems if we did not know that they were indeed written by Sanā'ī, and may very well have served him at any of the religious séances in which he was involved.[5]

More difficult to assess are a number of poems written by Sanā'ī for the Ghaznavid Sultan Bahrāmshāh (reigned 1118–ca. 1152). They are really ghazals, mostly describing a Beloved in terms which, though not explicitly mystical, are evidently referring to transcendent Beauty. To this, however, a brief panegyric has been attached marking the same ghazals as pieces of court poetry. This kind of ambiguity, in which the beloved (*ma'shūq*) not only seems to reflect the Divine (*ma'būd*) but also the person of a wordly patron (*mamdūḥ*), can be found with later poets as well, not least in the case of Ḥāfiẓ.[6]

Most important in Sanā'ī's ghazal poetry is the introduction of a cluster of antinomian themes centering on the figure of the 'qalandar', a tramp who flouts all the rules of good and pious behaviour, to which we will return later.

Among Sanā'ī's contemporaries Sayyid Ḥasan-i Ghaznavī (d. ab. 1160), also known under the name Ashraf, should be mentioned as an interesting early poet of the ghazal. He began his career as a court poet of Bahrāmshāh, but left Ghazna to travel to other places, especially in Western Persia and Khurasan. It is worthwhile noting that, apart from his literary fame, he acquired the additional reputations of a religious scholar and a very successful preacher.

In the twelfth century, prominent poets of the court like Anvarī (d. ca. 1165), Jamāl ad-Dīn Iṣfahānī (d. 1192) and Khāqānī (d. 1199) became interested in the writing of ghazals, although all three were celebrated writers of *qaṣīdas* in the first place. Many of their ghazals show the influence of Sanā'ī, even to the extent that a transcendental interpretation of their lyricism is by no means always excluded.

A truly mystical poet, who after Sanā'ī, deserves to be put into focus, was Farīd ad-Dīn 'Aṭṭār (d. ab. 1220). Very little is known with certainty about his life and mystical affiliations except that he earned a living as a pharmacist in the bazaar of Nishapur.[7] His *Dīvān* of lyrical poetry consists mainly of ghazals. According to Hellmut Ritter, who has analysed a great number of 'Aṭṭār's poems and compared some of them with Sanā'ī's ghazals, the mystical intention of the former is more outspoken than in the latter's poems.[8] What links the two poets together, in particular, is the importance they gave to antinomian motives. On the other hand, quite of few of his ghazals have the character of short poetic sermons rather than lyrics.

The name of Maulānā Jalāl ad-Dīn Rūmī (1207–73) is often mentioned as the third master of mystical poetry in a line including Sanā'ī and 'Aṭṭār and culminating in his work. He was born in Balkh which, until it was devastated by the Mongols, was one of the great centres of Islamic civilisation in eastern Persia (presently the northern part of Afghanistan). His father Bahā ad-Dīn Valad was a renowned theologian and preacher as well as a profound mystic.[9] When Jalāl ad-Dīn was still very young, his family travelled to the west settling down eventually in Konya, a city in Anatolia which in those days was still called Rūm. At the beginning he followed in the footsteps of his father; he became the revered teacher of a growing number of pupils. In 1244 an enigmatic dervish by the name of Shams ad-Dīn Tabrīzī turned up in Konya, who claimed to have reached the highest position imaginable in mystical love. His appearance made a crushing impact on Jalāl ad-Dīn. Shams ad-Dīn became not merely a very intimate companion, but actually an object of worship to him. These feelings were only heightened when in 1247 Shams suddenly left him. Rūmī sent his son Sulṭān Valad to Damascus to bring him back to Konya; but not for long, however, as a few months later he disappeared again, probably having been murdered by jealous people from Rūmī's own circle.

Many poems in the *Dīvān-i kabīr* ('The great Dīvān'), the huge collection of Rūmī's ghazals with more than 3,200 poems, give expression to his mystical relationship to Shams ad-Dīn. The latter's name is often mentioned in clasp themes, as in this indication of the true inspiration of Rūmī's poetry:

Behold, without regarding the letters, what is this language in the heart;
Pureness of colour is a quality derived from the Source of Action.
Shamsi Tabriz is seated in royal state, and before him
My rhymes are ranked like willing servants.[10]

This unique use of the device of personalisation betrays the intensity of Jalāl ad-Dīn's identification of Shams with the manifestation of the mystical Beloved in the flesh. These ghazals exhibit an almost inexhaustible wealth of imagery which is unparalleled in Persian literature.[11]

In the same century, Fakhr ad-Dīn 'Irāqī (d. 1289) made the most extensive use of the antinomistic theme, which since Sanā'ī and 'Aṭṭār had become fully integrated in the ghazal. With 'Irāqī, it acquired a special significance because it corresponded to the poet's actual way of life according to a biographical tradition which, although it certainly contains many legendary traits, may very well have a historical background. In his youth, he joined a group of antinomian dervishes when they passed through his native town Hamadan, having fallen in love with a boy who belonged to this group. Their wanderings brought him to Multan (presently in south-west Pakistan), where he entered the Chistī Order as an adept of the famous Shaykh Bahā ad-Dīn Zakarīyā. He continued to express himself in ecstatic poems using a highly offensive imagery, which eventually caused his expulsion from Multan. Returning to the Middle East, he settled down for some time in the Anatolian town of Konya. There he attended the teaching of Ṣadr ad-Dīn Qunavī, one of the earliest expounders of the mystical philosophy of Ibn al-ʻArabī. Inspired by the new theories about the 'Unity of Being', he wrote the *Lamaʻāt*, a treatise on the theory of love in the style of Aḥmad Gazālī's *Savāniḥ*. After a visit to Egypt he went to Damascus, where he died and was buried near the tomb of Ibn al-ʻArabī.[12]

The fame of Musharrif ad-Dīn ibn Muṣliḥ ad-Dīn Saʻdī (d. 1292 or 1294)[13] of Shiraz is, at least in Persia, based equally on his role as a poet of the ghazal as on the *Gulistān* and the *Būstān*, works which are best known to Western readers. Saʻdī collected his numerous ghazals into four collections which are known under the titles *Ṭayyibāt* ('Perfumed Poems'), *Badā'iʻ* ('Eloquent Poems'), *Khavātim* ('Sealed Poems') and *Ghazalīyāt-i qadīm* ('Old Ghazals'). Also with Saʻdī, the mystical intention is not in all poems self-evident, but this need not lead to the contrary conclusion. The Czech historian of Persian literature Jan Rypka cautioned: 'It is indeed not advisable to look for Sufism always and everywhere – either in Saʻdī or in other poets.'[14] There can be no doubt, however, that Saʻdī participated fully in the development of the ghazal which made the poem in the first place a vehicle of mystical emotions, or at least of an eroticism which is embedded in an awareness of its transcendental potential. Our knowledge about Saʻdī's life and his personality is almost entirely dependent on what he tells about himself in his works. He did not shrink from using biography as an element of fiction, describing journeys he never could have made or encounters with persons he could not have met. However, there is little reason to doubt the general picture of a man attracted to the life of a dervish, though not to the more extreme aspects of mysticism, and the kind of revered religiously minded person who deserved the nickname 'Sheikh' which the tradition has given to him.

Amīr Khusrau Dihlavī (1253–1325),[15] who was the son of a Turkish military man from Central Asia, became the first great poet of the Persian tradition in India. He spent his days as a courtier, mostly in Delhi, but was at the same time an intimate adept of Muḥammad Niẓām ad-Dīn Auliyā, a leading sheikh of the Chishtī Order. His biography, therefore, makes it quite obvious that mysticism must have been the main inspiration of his ghazals. He collected his lyrical work in no less than five albums. Their titles reveal that Khusrau saw them as the reflection of stages in a progress towards inner purification and perfection marked by the various stages of his life: *Tuḥfat aṣ-ṣighar* ('The Present of Youth'), *Vasaṭ al-ḥayāt* ('The Middle of Life'), *Ghurrat al-kamāl* ('Dawn of Perfection'), *Bāqiya-yi nāqiya* ('The Pure Remainder') and *Nihāyat al-kamāl* ('Final Perfection').

A scholar of Islamic law, who at the same time was heir to a local mystical tradition, was 'Imād ad-Dīn (1291–1371),[16] nicknamed Faqīh-i Kirmānī, 'the jurisprudent of Kirmān'. At an early age he succeeded his father as the director of a Sufi convent. As he relates in one of his *masnavī* poems – to which we shall return in the next chapter – he wrote ghazals to be recited during the gatherings held in this convent.

Another mystic of the same period was Khvājū Kirmānī (1290–1352 or 1361),[17] a member of the Kāzarūnī Order in the southern province of Fars. As as a poet of ghazals he followed in the footsteps of Sa'dī, although he is best known for his *masnavīs*. Salmān-i Sāvajī (d. 1376), on the other hand, was first of all a court poet serving the Mongol dynasty of the Jalā'irids at Baghdad. He is regarded as the last medieval master of the *qaṣīda*, which he applied to religious panegyrics of the Prophet and 'Alī. He is also, however, appreciated as a writer of mystical ghazals, whose use of imagery has been compared to the style of Ḥāfiẓ.

Ḥāfiẓ (d. ab. 1390)[18] is by universal consent the greatest Persian poet of ghazals. His poetry poses the problem of the distinction between the profane and the mystical in its most acute form. The question has been discussed over and again in modern times, not only by Western critics, but equally by Persian scholars, and as yet no unanimity has been reached. Also in this case, biography is an important issue in the argumentation. Like his older fellow townsman Sa'dī, he was in touch with the local court of Shiraz, at least during most of his active life. Traces of his contacts with rulers and courtiers have been found in his poems in the form of panegyrical references. Some of them are of an allusive nature and their interpretation therefore remains uncertain. It is evident, however, that Ḥāfiẓ, like Sanā'ī and others did before him, wrote several panegyrical ghazals, mentioning the name of his patron at the end of the poem.

Against all this it could be held that Ḥāfiẓ makes an intensive use of all the images and motives which, for centuries already, belonged to the stock-in-trade of the mystical ghazal. Most Oriental commentators of previous centuries have given mystical readings of his poetry. The matter is further confused by the kaleidoscopic nature of Ḥāfiẓ' verse. In any given poem one may find a great variety of elements, some of them pointing in the direction of a transcendental meaning, others allowing the possibility of a secular interpretation.

During the thirteenth and fourteenth centuries, when the two great masters of Shiraz lived, the ghazal was firmly established as the most important Persian lyrical form, and it kept this position for many centuries. In the period immediately following, its character as a mystical poem became much more outspoken. Many poets were Sufi sheikhs in the first place, and made use of the ghazal as a means to express their teachings in imaginative language. At the centre of their poetry stands the theosophical doctrine of Ibn al-'Arabī (d. 1240) on the 'Unity of Being' (*waḥdat al-wujūd*), which had become predominant in Sufism. The poetry of love, which gave words to the yearning for unity with the Beloved, lent itself easily for the formulation of the awareness of existential unity. Yet, there was an unmistakable shift from the expression of emotional states to a more intellectual attitude.

Kamāl ad-Dīn Mas'ūd, better known as Kamāl-i Khujandī (d. ca. 1405) was born in Central Asia but spent most of his life in Tabriz. Sultan Ḥusayn Jalā'irī, who was the Mongol ruler of

Western Persia in his days, gave him a garden and a convent where he could teach. This is only one of many signs of the great interest that men of worldly power took in Sufism. Kamāl's poetry is said to have exerted an influence on Ḥāfiẓ's.[19]

A contemporary of Kamāl, who also lived in Tabriz, was Maulānā Muḥammad Maghribī (d. 1406–7), nicknamed Shīrīn ('The sweet'). He derived his name from his investiture with the Sufi cloak (*khirqa*) which was performed by a sheikh during a journey of the poet to North Africa. In spite of his high rank as a mystic, Maghribī also had good relations with Mīrānshāh, the Timurid governor of Adharbayjan, who for some time was his pupil.[20] The great Sufi sheikh Shāh Ni'mat-Allāh Valī (d. 1431), founder of the Ni'matallāhī Order (one of the main Sufi traditions of Persia and India), was born in a family of Sayyids from Aleppo, Syria, which had settled down in the Persian city of Kirman. He was also a prolific writer of ghazals.[21] Qāsim-i Anvār (d. 1433) entertained relations with Ṣafī ad-Dīn, the sheikh of the Ṣafavid Sufi Order in Ardabil (Adharbayjan) from which in the sixteenth century emerged the first Shi'ite dynasty governing the whole of Persia. Qāsim is also known as a writer of *masnavīs*.[22]

Maulānā Nūr ad-Dīn 'Abd ar-Raḥman Jami (1414–92), was a leading sheikh of the Naqshbandī Order, the dominant Sufi organisation at the court of the Timurids in Herat. He left an enormous *oeuvre* containing virtually all the genres, in prose as well as in poetry, which had been current in the previous centuries. His collection of hagiographies, *Nafaḥāt al-Uns*, is an important source for the history of Sufism and includes a section on mystical poets. His lyrics, including many ghazals, were assembled in three volumes, according to the stages of his life, following the example set by Amīr Khusrau of Dihlī: *Fātiḥat ash-shabāb* ('The beginning of youth'), *Vāsiṭat al-'iqd* ('The middle pearl of the necklace'), and *Khātimat al-ḥayāt* ('The seal of life'). The influence of Jami exceeded the boundaries of Persian poetry and is noticeable in the Persian-style poetry of classical Ottoman-Turkish literature.[23]

Of the numerous other ghazal poets at least Bābā Fighānī (d. about 1500) should be mentioned, because he made a strong impact on ghazal poetry in the Safavid period.[24] The mystical ghazal continued to be important during the subsequent centuries, especially in the works of the poets who belonged to the school of the so-called 'Indian style'. Their most prominent representative in Persia was Ṣā'ib of Tabriz (d. 1676), whose tremendous output exhibits the use of the poetic possibilities of the ghazal at a rare height of complexity.[25] Even in the twentieth century, Muḥammad-Ḥusayn Shahriyār (d. 1988), the greatest modern master of the ghazal, could breathe new life into this ancient form of mystical poetry.[26]

The scope of ghazal poetry

If it is true that the mystical Persian ghazal had its origin in songs about earthly love, the basic elements among its stock of images and motives must be those which betray that peculiar background most clearly. These were the features which attracted the attention of the mystics in the first place, when they adopted this kind of secular poetry. It should be kept in mind, however, that even profane ghazals were much more than simple love songs. Also earthly love is a complex of acts, relationships and emotions which cannot be expressed in plain words but requires the help of the poetic imagination to deal with such intangibles. Even a purely physical topic like the beautiful appearance of the beloved person cannot be described without having recourse to figurative language and poetic imagery because only in that way can the lover show how this beauty affects his soul.

To the ghazal poet, Nature in particular is full of analogies to his experiences in love. He finds them in particular in the season of Spring, when the rebirth of nature provides the strongest impulses to his imagination. A garden in full vernal flower is an almost inexhaustible source of symbolic references to perfect beauty and, thereby, to the beauty of the poet's idol. The cypress, which in Persian was said to be a 'free' tree, represented the slim, elegant stature of the admired person whereas red flowers like tulips and roses provided the equivalent of blushing cheeks, the hyacinth or the violet of curly locks and the narcissus of the dreamy eyes. In a ghazal, Ḥasan-i Ghaznavī elaborated the idea of the analogy between love and nature. The flowers remind him of his Beloved:

The fragrant rose blossoms in the garden;
It seems to me, this is the face of my Fairest.
The tulip in the green meadow appears to the eye
As the face of the Beloved sitting beside me.
From afar, the intoxicated narcissus
Is my Sweetheart's eye looking out for me.
When I see the violets, I say to myself:
'These are his locks, or else my emaculated body.'

These are only the most conspicuous items of this imaginative language which, at the time when mystical poets adopted it, had already become stereotyped to such a degree that a 'walking cypress' was hardly felt as a figurative reference to the beloved anymore.

The animal kingdom provided an equally rich repertoire. The famous nightingale who, as the partner of the rose, stands for the poet-lover, is only one of a great variety of items. Sayyid Ḥasan identified himself with three different birds in the opening section of the same ghazal:

In Spring the turtle-dove is my companion
Who joins in with my bitter complaints.
The ring-dove wears the ring of Love around his neck
Pining for the friend who could relief my pain.
The nightingale can be heard from the rosebush
Expressing faithfully my miserable lot.

If we add to this the many features derived from the mineral world (like 'ruby lips', and 'teeth like pearls') and the heavenly spheres with their stars and planets (e.g. Sun and Moon as tropes for a shining face), a complete picture of the universe emerges, in which all the layers of being distinguished by the medieval view of the world are represented. This cosmos of poetic imagery mirrors not merely the perfect beauty of the beloved, but also the exalted feelings evoked by love itself. Obviously, there exists no more than a formal relationship with the real world: this is an idealised world, more akin to the visualisation of Paradise as it is well-known to a Muslim audience from the Koran. However, there was a significant difference. Unlike Paradise, the beauty of the poetic garden of spring is ephemeral; it has as a counterpart the decay of the autumnal garden, in which the flowers and blossoming trees have lost their verdure, and the songs of the nightingale have made way for the screeches of the crow. This contrast equally provides an opportunity for symbolism. The excitement created by the coming of spring alternates with the disillusionment brought about by the death of nature or, expressed in the terms of love itself, the joyful experience of 'union' is followed inevitably by the pain of 'separation'.

Apart from nature, social life is reflected in Persian ghazals as well. In many poems the environment which is understood (if not actually pictured) is a convivial gathering where the poet indulges in wine-drinking with his friends. Usually, when he calls out to the cup-bearer for a drink, a motivation is added. This may be no more than the celebration of the coming of spring, which one cannot enjoy without wine, but often it has a more melancholy note when the poet seeks comfort in intoxication for the pain caused by his love, for the wrongs afflicted by the World or the inexorable passing of Time. Even in secular poems, wine therefore may adopt the figurative meaning of a means of escape from a cruel reality into a realm of hope and illusions about the fulfilment of love.

The essential theme of a ghazal is, of course, love itself. In the last analysis, this theme consists of a triangle in which three actors play their separate parts: the Lover, the Beloved, and Love in as far as this concept can be abstracted from the persons involved. An etymological link between the partners in this triangle is provided by the Arabic root *'ayn-shīn-qāf* which respectively produces the words *'āshiq*, 'the Lover', *ma'shūq*, 'the Beloved', and *'ishq*, 'Love' itself.

The Lover is represented by the lyrical *persona* of the poet. That is, the 'I' who speaks in the poems. In clasp themes, however, the speaking voice usually distinguishes itself from the poet by addressing him or talking about him as if he were an absent third person. An introspective division is made within the speaking person when he turns to his own heart, which is the seat of the emotions produced by love.

The second actor, the Beloved, is the person who is either described or addressed by the Lover. As a rule this person remains anonymous and is only indicated by pronouns of the second or third person. As the Persian language has no distinction of gender in pronouns, the sex of the Beloved is very often not indicated. There is much more to this than a linguistic peculiarity, because it marks the very special character of the ghazal as an erotic poem and therefore needs some explanation. If one were to judge solely on the majority of these poems, where there is no clue as to the gender of the Beloved, the conclusion could be drawn that the Persian ghazal is concerned with love at a level where the distinction between the sexes has become irrelevant. Up to a certain extent, this conclusion is valid because the lyricism of the ghazal does indeed transcend eroticism in its mundane sense, even in poems which cannot be labelled as mystical.

However, the fact cannot be overlooked that, in quite a few cases, indications of gender do occur; some of them even belong to the most characteristic motifs of this poetry. Such indications point nearly always to the male gender of the Beloved. There is a remarkable difference in this respect with Persian narrative poetry, in which pairs of lovers (like Majnūn and Lailā, Khusrau and Shīrīn or Yūsuf and Zulaykhā) are nearly always heterosexual, the female partner usually playing the role of the Beloved. Also in Arabic love poetry, the Beloved is female as a rule and, moreover, not anonymous.

In order to place this feature of the Persian ghazal in its proper perspective, the setting to which the love relationships described in this poetry refer to should be considered. The environment alluded to is, both socially and conceptually, the atmosphere of male entertainment in gatherings to which the general term of *majlis* (literally 'a place where one sits together') was applied. Perhaps this is the main reason why the Beloved is very often specified as a young man. Sometimes, he is addressed as a 'boy' (*pisar*) or he can be identified as one of male servants in such gatherings, in particular as the cup-bearer (*sāqī*). Ethnic specifications also occur: one of the most frequently used is 'Turk', by which we should think of a palace-slave or a young soldier, for in both functions Turkish young men commonly served at medieval Persian courts.

Another unmistakable indication is the mention of a beard, in particular of the first signs of its growth on the cheeks of an adolescent. This became a favourite motif in the ghazals as it could be used as the starting point of the expression of the blended feelings of sadness and desire: the former, because it signalled the end of youth, and the latter, because it showed the same face at the apex of its pristine beauty, just as the moon is most perfect at the very moment when its decline sets in.

The convention of love poetry as it embodied in ghazals prescribes certain rules for the description of the Beloved. The description of physical beauty is concentrated on the head, encompassing both the face and the hair. Eyes, lips and cheeks are prominent features of the former but also the lower part of the ear and the chin with its dimple belong to this conventional catalogue. As far as the hair is concerned, its blackness, symbolising distancing and concealment, and the curls, which are the image of the devious ways of the Beloved, receive special attention.

A fundamental function assigned to the Beloved in ghazal poetry is that of being a *shāhid*, a 'witness', namely of a transcendent Beauty. The latter manifests itself in all things of beauty to be found among the world's phenomena. As a concept it stems from the great impact of Platonism on medieval Islamic culture; poetically, it provides a justification for the use of erotic motives in mystical poetry: the description of a lover's infatuation with the earthly Beloved loses its objectionable features when the higher perspective of the love for the eternal, imperishable Beloved is brought into play.

The third actor in this triangle, Love itself, can be singled out as an entity in its own right because it is quite often a separate theme of a ghazal; some ghazals are didactical poems dealing with abstract considerations and not with erotic emotions.

The psychology of a love relationship is elaborated in a great number of themes. A catalogue was drawn up by Kay-Kā'ūs, quoted earlier, in the advice he gave to the minstrels who, at least in the eleventh century, were pre-eminently the performers of love poetry. He starts by warning of a too personal use of love poetry:

> *If it so happens that you are in love with someone, do not speak every day about your own situation for, though it may be sweet to hear to yourself, it is not so to others. Choose a different subject for each song. Learn a lot of poems and ghazals by heart, for instance about separation, reunion, reproach (*taubīkh*), criticism (*malāmat*), chastising (*'itāb*), rejection, refusal, acceptation, cruelty, faithfulness, presents, magnanimity, contentment; or about situations at certain moments and in certain seasons, like poems for springtime, autumn, summer and winter.*[27]

Among these subjects the complaints about the absence, the indifference or the cruelty of the Beloved towards the Lover by far outweigh the expression of elated feelings caused by the fulfilment of the Lover's desire. It should also be noted that these various themes were not appreciated as the expression of personal experience but rather as the representation of Love in its general aspects.

The ghazal as a mystical poem

The adoption of the ghazal by the Sufi poets should be interpreted as a borrowing from a secular and well-established tradition of love poetry, which originally belonged to Persian court literature.[28] The history of this process is difficult to trace in all its detail because it must have started already long before the time of the oldest datable specimens known to us. It is certain, however, that the mystics of Islam were almost from the very beginning fascinated by the theme of Love as one of the most appropriate metaphors of their relationship with the Divine. Early mystical love poetry in Arabic are the lines attributed to the female mystic Rābi'a who lived in the late eigth century.[29]

The preoccupation with erotic metaphors was not only a literary phenomenon, but can also be found in rituals of the Sufis which were equally imitated from the ways of the world. Under the name of *samā'*, which literally means 'hearing', a complex of artistic forms practised by the Sufis is subsumed: it comprises music, dance and the recitation of poetry. Their integration into Sufi practice was undoubtedly problematic, as they were derived from the type of secular conviviality which was most objectionable to Islamic piety. The question whether, from the point of view of Islamic law, these practices were permitted or not was often discussed. In the early twelfth century, very influential spiritual leaders like the brothers Aḥmad and Muḥammad Ghazālī defended these practices, though not without certain restrictions which were to prevent such expressions of mystical ectasy from becoming entangled with the sinful promptings of the lower soul. According to Muḥammad Ghazālī, the aesthetic enjoyment of music and song could be helpful to kindle the innate 'fire' which God had hidden in the human heart. To him whose heart is in the grip of the love of God, the ritual of the *samā'* may even be said to be necessary as a means to strengthen the flames of his love. On the other hand, the sensuality inherent in these artistic expressions creates an obvious danger to all who practise them. The answer to the question of their permissibility in mysticism is bound therefore to the criterium of the intention. The *samā'* brings out nothing more than what is hidden already in the heart. Its purity depends entirely on the degree of purification which has already been realised by the participant. Even under that condition, the ritual should be carefully regulated in order to avoid any influence of sinful motives.[30]

Another area where the impact of love poetry made itself felt was the type of popular preaching which under the name of *va'ẓ*, is distinguished from the more formal *khuṭbas*, the sermons which were held during the Friday prayers. Muslim preachers who used erotic poetry to arouse the religious emotions of their audience also became the target of severe criticism by strict theologians.[31]

The ideas about the meaning of love in mysticism which were current in medieval Islam found a basis in several strains of theoretical thought. Scholastic psychology acknowledged the attachment of the specifically human, or rational, soul to lower strata, which were called the vegetative and the animal souls. From this model, the doctrine of the realisation of the human potential through the subjection of these lower impulses to the control by the rational soul was derived. Hellenistic traditions provided the Platonic concept of *erôs* as the principal drive of all created beings towards their Creator. Within the civilisation of Islam a specific theory of love emerged, first in Arabic literature and since the early twelfth century also in Persian prose works. The first treatise of this kind was the earlier cited *Savāniḥ* ('Flashes'), written by Aḥmad Ghazālī in an extremely subtle style, which was most suitable for the intricacies of its subject. The author's aim was to maintain a perfect balance between the secular and mystical concepts of love, avoiding carefully any choice between one side or the other. However, it is quite obvious that Aḥmad Ghazālī's real interest was in sublimated love. This short essay is of the greatest importance to a more fundamental understanding of ghazal poetry and the psychology of the loving soul which constitutes the basis of this poetry. Other writers who followed Ghazālī's example, explicitly stated their mystical intentions. Mention should be made of the *Lavā'iḥ*,('Splendours'), a work attributed, probably mistakenly, to 'Ayn al-Quẓāt Hamadānī (d. 1131), *'Abhar al-'āshiqīn* ('The Narcissus of the Lovers') by Rūzbihān-i Baqlī (d. 1128–1209), a mystic of Shiraz, and the *Mu'nis al-'ushshāq* ('The Companion of the Lovers') by the mystical philosopher Shihāb ad-Dīn Yaḥyā Suhravardī, nicknamed al-Maqtūl, because he was executed in 1191 on the accusation of heresy. To be added is 'Irāqī's *Lama'āt* ('Flashes'), a work by an important ghazal poet who has been mentioned above.

The mystical poetry of love itself also became a subject of theoretical consideration. Lists were drawn up to explain the manifold motives used by the poets in terms of mystical thought. In such catalogues of Sufi vocabulary, the images were more or less mummified as items of a fixed code which could be decoded into a series of abstract notions. This undoubtedly robbed them of their vitality and flexibility as items of an imaginative discourse. An early source showing this tendency is the *Mirṣād al-'ibād* by Najm al-Dīn Dāya (d. 1256), an influential textbook of Sufi ideas on the development of the human soul, which is not only rich in poetic citations, but uses itself a style marked by the abundance of poetical imagery. At least from the fourteenth century onwards, the idiom of poetry had become fully integrated into the language normally used in Sufi writings. A good example of the process of the incorporation of poetical imagery in a more or less formalized terminology is provided by the celebrated *Gulshan-i rāz* of Maḥmūd Shabistarī, written in 1317.[32] In this tiny didactical poem Shabistarī gave interpretations to a number of well-known images from ghazal poetry, mainly taken from the poems of Farīd ad-Dīn 'Aṭṭār. His work has been extremely popular throughout the subsequent centuries and has certainly been very influential in shaping the Sufi terminology as it became known in later times. It was explained in a long series of commentaries, the outstanding work among which was Shams ad-Dīn Lāhijī's *Miftāḥ al-i'jāz*, written about 1471. As it exceeds many times the basic text it constitutes a mystical treatise in its own right.

Unbelievers and qalandars

The plight of the true lover is full of paradoxes. Although love leads the soul on to the highest bliss imaginable, the road to be followed is a particularly rough one and leads through an abyss of self-denial and humiliation. The experience of love is often a very painful one. However, such pain should not be avoided but be welcomed as a sign of the beloved's attention. Love is a way of gaining knowledge about the desired object; not by reason, but through a form of intuitive perception often designated as *z̲auq* ('taste'). There is also a contradiction in a moral sense. To be really in love amounts to focusing completely on the Beloved without any regard for one's own well-being, even to the point of accepting annihilation through love. At this elevated stage of self-denial the common standards of moral and religious behaviour have become irrelevant. Distinctions between good and bad, or belief and unbelief, are not binding any more on the lover. They refer to values tinged by expectations of reward and salvation that are concerned with the lover's self-interest, and therefore point to aims other than the unconditional surrender to the Beloved's sovereign will.

These fundamental characteristics of love are all reflected in Persian ghazals. As we saw, the search for a perception beyond the boundaries of rational thinking is expressed by various motives related to the drinking of wine. The sufferings caused by the elusiveness of the Beloved and the rejection of the lover's advances are willingly accepted even if many poems are filled with complaints about the dismal condition of lovers. The most striking feature is, however, the open confession by the lover of his being an unbeliever and his disregard of values and rules of conduct which are sacred to the pious Muslim. Mystical ghazals abound with jibes at devout ascetics who keep vigils, fast and recite the Koran in their cells. The point of this criticism is that Sufis who only care for their good name in this world and salvation in the afterlife ignore their true mystical calling, which is the state of love. Like other representatives of official religion, such as divine scholars and preachers, they are under the suspicion of pursuing merely a selfish aim by showing off their piety and thereby soliciting the people's veneration.

The antinomian motives which became such a conspicuous element of mystical ghazals can be linked to a parallel phenomenon in the history of Sufism. In the ninth century a reaction to the predominantly ascetic orientation of the early Sufi sheikhs arose in the eastern Persian province of Khurasan. This tendency became known as the *malāmatīya*, after the central concept of *malāmat* ('blame'). By this, a concern was inferred about the motives behind the commonly practised piety, which was suspected of being no more than 'showing off piety' (*riyā*) directed towards the world. In order to counter this serious danger for the mystical soul the reverse attitude was advocated, namely a behaviour that elicits criticism rather than admiration. The mystic should not only conceal his acts of devotion from the eyes of the people, but should actually behave in such a manner that he becomes the object of their disapproval. The intention of this was to purge love of insincerity. However, the school of blame itself did not remain above criticism. Hujvīrī (d. ca. 1075), an early Persian writer on the theory of Sufism, who admitted that blame had 'a great effect in making love sincere', also pointed out that it might end up in the very position which it tried to avoid:

> *The ostentatious man purposely acts in such a way as to win popularity, while the Malámatí purposely acts in such a way that the people reject him. Both have their thoughts fixed on mankind and do not pass beyond that sphere.*[33]

In spite of this, the antinomian way continued to attract many who strove after a total renunciation both in their behaviour and their spirituality. From the thirteenth century onwards various groups of dervishes are known who used their blameworthy conduct as a shield against worldly attachments in whatever form. Their scandalising behaviour distinguished them sharply from 'mainstream' Sufism as it was organised and disciplined within the framework of the mystical orders.[34] Nevertheless, the concept of blame as such could be accepted by orthodox Sufis as a respectable attitude as long as it was restricted to a concealment of spiritual virtues which served as a safeguard for the sincerity of the mystic's devotion. Abū Ḥafṣ 'Umar as-Suhrawardī (1144–1234), who was the founder of one of the largest Sufi orders, commented favourably on the Malāmatīya in his *'Awārif al-ma'ārif* ('Gifts of Insights'), an authoritative textbook of moderate Sufism. However, he strongly condemned those who imagined that, for the sake of the 'well-being of the heart' (*ṭībat al-qalb*), they were free to break all the rules of good and pious behaviour. To distinguish them from the former group, Suhrawardī used the term Qalandarīya to denote the latter tendency, but it is not clear whether he meant a specific community actually existing under that name.[35] Historically, it is uncertain whether groups using this name existed in the early thirteenth century.[36]

Another uncertainty pertains to the relationship between this phenomenon in the history of Islamic mysticism on the one hand, and Sufi poetry on the other. The earliest use of the word *qalandar* in mystical texts predates its use as a designation for a particular type of dervish by a long time. The first instances may even go back to the eleventh century, although they are not quite reliable specimens as they occur in the collections of quatrains attributed to Bābā Ṭāhir and Abū Sa'īd, the uncertain authenticity of which we have discussed before. In the same period, a *Qalandar-nāma* would have been written if it could be proven that the mystic 'Abd-Allāh Anṣārī (d. 1089) was really the author as the textual tradition claims. In this little prose text it is told how a *qalandar* suddenly appears in a theological school. He convinces the students to abandon their books and follow him to what is called 'the place of the chains' (*zanjīrgāh*, by which perhaps a madhouse is meant) where he preaches to them on the real demands of a mystical life.[37]

More solid ground is reached at the beginning of the next century when reliable evidence is available. Aḥmad Ghazālī (d. 1126) illustrates in his *Savāniḥ* the consequences of *malāmat* to the lover by citing this quatrain:

This is the lane of blame, the field of annihilation;
This is the street where gamblers put all at one stake.
The courage of a qalandar, clothed in rags, is needed
To pass through in a bold and fearless manner.

It is debatable whether one should regard the poems which were eventually called *qalandarīyāt*, as a separate poetic genre. Although there are indeed many instances of poems entirely devoted to this motif, it also occurs in connection with other elements, especially in the ghazals. Perhaps it is better to regard *qalandarīyāt* as the name of a cluster of imagery applied to the theme of blame as one of the basic elements of love. Aḥmad Ghazālī gave much weight to it in his theoretical exposition. He compared *malāmat* to a sword by which love should be trimmed until it is reduced to its very essence: first blame manifests itself in the beloved's jealousy which prevents the lover from looking at others; then the jealousy of the 'moment', that is the ecstasy of love, turns the lover away from himself; in the end, love's own jealousy forces the lover to abandon all desire, even for his own beloved, and concentrate on nothing else but love.[38]

It is this total commitment to love to which the antinomian motives in ghazal poetry refer. One should therefore take care not to read a reflection of reality in these poetic images. Poets such as Sanā'ī (d. 1131) and Farīd ad-Dīn 'Aṭṭār (d. ca. 1220), who used them very frequently in their poetry, were certainly not antinomian mystics, but pious Muslims who put much emphasis on the obedience to God's will as it was laid down in the *sharī'at*. Only in the case of 'Irāqī (d. 1289) it may be assumed that there was indeed a relationship between letters and life, that is if we trust the hagiographical tradition that grew up around him. After all, 'Irāqī lived in a period when antinomian mysticism first appeared as a prominent element in Islamic societies.

The central figure, from whom the cluster received its name, is the *qalandar*; sometimes he is also called *qallāsh*. The origin of both words is unknown and so is the real-life model on which the poets moulded their qalandars. In one of the oldest specimens, a quatrain quoted in an anecdote by Abū Sa'īd's biographer Ibn al-Munavvar, the qalandar is depicted as a tramp playing on a half-broken instrument and begging for wine.[39] He is an outcast whose favourite dwelling-place is the *kharābāt*. Literally this means 'ruins'; the connotation of a 'tavern' or 'brothel', frequented by debauched persons like the qalandars, is a feature taken from reality because such places were often situated in delapidated parts of medieval cities. However, the name could easily be used in a metaphorical sense as well: living in 'ruins' amounted to being in the material world which is full of decay. The attitude of the tramp, symbolising the rejection of any attachment to this world, is the right one in such abject surroundings. This lifestyle is sometimes presented as a 'rite' (*ā'īn*). The prescriptions are to indulge in all things forbidden. In addition to drinking and sexual excesses, gambling with dice, backgammon or chess is frequently mentioned. The qalandar, the person who puts all on one stake, is the perfect example of the lover who is totally committed to his passion. The *kharābāt* can be pictured as the temple of an imaginary cult exhibiting elements taken from non-Muslim religions, in particular Christianity and Zoroastrianism. To enter this community one should bind oneself with the *zunnār*, the sign Christians living under Muslim rule were obliged to wear, but at the same time representing the *kushtī*, the girdle bound three times around the middle as a token of the initiation in the Zoroastrian religion. The object of the cult is fire or wine; the officiating priest is called *pīr-i mughān* ('Elder of the Magi'). His tool is the *jām-i Jam*, the cup said to have been used by the mythical king Jamshīd to forecast the future at the Iranian New Year festival.[40]

In this strange looking glass religion the norms and values of Sufi piety are all reversed. The 'Elder of the Magi' is the counterpart of the Sufi Master and the jibes at the ascetic way of life which we mentioned earlier are an essential part of its repertoire. Once the underlying theme of *malāmat* is recognised, however, the real intention behind this masque is not difficult to grasp. The cult of the 'Magi', in spite of its apparel of debauchery and unbelief, represents nothing but the pursuit of the purged state which is the prerequisite of an unconditional surrender to mystical love. The cup, which is often equated to a mirror, stands for the human heart, the organ for the communication with the Unseen by way of intuitive knowledge.

A specimen from the ghazals of Ḥāfiẓ

The stylistic development of Persian ghazals in the course of its long history is a subject which cannot possibly be dealt with here properly. It should be admitted that the subject itself still escapes the grip of literary scholarship, and it will continue to do so until the time when the works of at least the most important masters of the ghazal will have been investigated in sufficient detail. The main obstacles facing the researcher are the enormous size of the material to be studied, the length of the tradition and, above all, the fact that, over the centuries, the poetic language and the stock of imagery and motives used in these poems appear to have undergone very little change. In order to describe a development of style, which undoubtedly must have taken place, one has to examine closely the interplay of all these linguistic and literary elements within the works of successive generations of poets.

Nevertheless, a few general lines of development can easily be detected, and have been mentioned in critical studies with a considerable degree of unanimity. The most important of these is the trend towards a greater concentration in the application of the conventional elements of ghazal poetry. By the fourteenth century, this development had advanced to a remarkable degree. In Ḥāfiẓ's ghazals, in particular, a kaleidoscopical density of imagery can be found which presents a major problem to the interpretation of the works of this often elusive poet. Several studies have focused on the question of whether or not it is possible to find the rules of composition lending unity to the seemingly random sequence of images and lyrical motives in a typical Ḥāfiẓean poem. A.J. Arberry, borrowing a line from the eighteenth century translator William Jones, has subsumed this question in the phrase 'Oriental pearls at random strung'. Denying the view, sometimes held by Western scholars, that these ghazals show little internal coherence, Arberry argued that it is indeed possible to see the links between a number of themes in one of Ḥāfiẓ's most famous poems.

To demonstrate the peculiarity of Ḥāfiẓ's style we examine here another specimen, namely a poem which is not only illustrative of the shifting imagery in the art of Ḥāfiẓ, but also of his use of mystical motifs. As we want to adhere as closely as possible to his original words, no attempt is made at a 'literary' translation; instead, a presentation of the Persian text in transcription is followed by a more or less literal paraphrase in English prose which, of course, cannot provide any impression of the aesthetic values of the original.

The poem (number 79 in the edition by P.N. Khānlarī) is a ghazal of eight lines and opens with a piece of nature poetry:

bulbulī barg-i gulī khush-rang dar minqār dāsht
v-andar-ān barg-u navā khush nālahā-yi zār dāsht
guftam-ash dar 'ayn-i vaṣl īn nāla-u faryād chīst
guft mā-rā jilva-yi ma'shūq dar īn kār dāsht

'A nightingale holding a colourful rose petal in his bill/ uttered bitter complaints in the midst of these riches.// I said to him: 'Why this complaining and lamenting when you have reached unity itself?'/ He said: 'It was the revelation of the beloved which made me do this!'.

If they are isolated from the rest of the poem, these lines form a unit enclosed within itself comparable to the tight structure of a quatrain: a little scene (the highly conventional picture of the nightingale singing to the rose) elicits an exchange of words between the poet and the bird, the outcome of which is an explanation of the paradox between the possession of the rose petal and the song of the nightingale, who continues to express his longing for the rose. There are two motifs mentioned which point to the meaning of these lines as parts of a more extensive composition dealing with ghazal themes and, therefore, contain the clue to tracing their connection to the rest of the poem. The first is marked by the use of the word *vaṣl*, 'unity', or 'unification' with the beloved, which on the list of Kay Kā'ūs cited above was mentioned among the principal themes of a love poem. The other is *jilva-yi ma'shūq*, the 'manifestation of the beloved'. To the nightingale, the rose petal is not the rose itself but merely points to the beauty of the latter, which is still unattainable to him. The manifestation by means of not more than a petal is really no more than a 'witness' of the transcendental beauty. Instead of fulfilling the bird's desire, the possession of the rose petal only heightens the pain of his love.

yār agar nanshast bā mā nīst jāy-i i'tirāẓ
pādishāhī kāmrān būd az gadāyān 'ār dāsht
dar namīgīrad niyāz-u nāz-i mā bā ḥusn-i dūst
khurram ān k-az nāzanīnān bakht barkhurdār dāsht

If the companion did not sit down with us, there is no reason to protest:/he was a mighty ruler who felt ashamed by the beggars.// Our prayers and our flattery have no effect on the beauty of the friend;/happy is he who found his luck with the coquettes.

The poet's voice goes on to consider the reasons why the Beloved behaves in such an evasive way, changing over to the image of the king who shuns the company of beggars. He stresses the uselessness of the lover's begging. He may regard himself as lucky if he is treated to the whims of the coquette beauties of this world who as 'witnesses' of the eternal Beloved play their games with the helpless lover.

khīz tā bar kilk-i ān naqqāsh jān-afshān kunīm
k-īn hama naqsh-i 'ajab dar gardish-i pargār dāsht

Arise! Let's offer our lives to the pen of that painter/who conjured all these wonderful images within the compass of the circle.

Here, a significant turning is made in two respects. Grammatically, the poet changes over to the imperative, that is he addresses his audience exhorting them to a total commitment to the cause of love. Further, there is a difference of orientation in as far as an unquestionably religious motif is brought into play. Behind the image of the painter hides the Divine Creator to Whom all the wordly beauties (i.e. the 'coquettes') owe their existence.

gar murīd-i rāh-i 'ishqī fikr-i badnāmī makun
shaykh-i Ṣan'ān khirqa rahn-i khāna-yi khammār dāsht
vaqt-i ān shīrīn qalandar khush ki dar aṭvār-i sayr
ẕikr-i tasbīḥ-i malak dar ḥalqa-yi zunnār dāsht

If you are an adept of the path of love, don't care about a bad reputation:/the sheikh from Ṣan'ān pawned his habit in the house of the wineseller.// Blessed are the hours of the sweetvoiced Qalandar who wherever he roamed,/ continued to praise God like the angels using the belt of his unbelief as a rosary.

The consideration of the lover's duty to submit himself completely to his Beloved's will brings the poet almost automatically to antinomian themes. The true follower of the Path of Love is equal to the *qalandar* dervish who is eager to sacrify his good name as a pious Muslim for the sake of his total submission to the Beloved. As Farīd ad-Dīn 'Aṭṭār tells in his *Manṭiq aṭ-ṭayr* ('The Conference of the Birds'), the Sheikh of Ṣan'ān was a pious Sufi master living in Mecca. When he was tempted by the love of a Christian girl he forsook his piety altogether to become her slave and commit all that was forbidden by Islam. This descent into a sinful life, however, rescued him from the false self-esteem which was the last obstacle on his road toward the mystical goal.[41] In this manner, the *zunnār*, the belt worn by Christians as a sign of their inferior status, could serve him as a rosary in an angelic commemoration of the Divine Name.

chashm-i Ḥāfiẓ zīr-i bām-i qaṣr-i ān Ḥūrī-sirisht
shīva-yi 'jannāt tajrī taḥtahā al-anhār' dāsht

Under the palace-roof of the one with the nature of a maiden of Paradise Ḥāfiẓ's eyes/ were enthralled by the 'Gardens under which the rivers flow'.

With this clasp-theme the poem culminates in a suggestion of paradise, quoting even directly from the Koran.[42] There can be no doubt that his statement encompasses love in all its aspects. The change of the imagery, ranging from a scene in an earthly garden to a glimpse of Paradise, helps the poet to talk about so much in so few words. He tells about the inaccessibility of the Beloved, of the manifestations of the absent One which are open to the eyes of the lover everywhere in the world; he refers to the demands put upon the true lover. There are, finally, several references to religious concepts like the dependence of the world on its Creator, the attitude of antinomian mystics and eternal happiness. Yet, in the final analysis, the question lingers on whether he talks about the supernatural only for its own sake, or still manages to keep the balance suspended between the sacred and the profane. Even if the possibility of such an ambiguity is left open, it could still be maintained that Ḥāfiẓ fulfilled the fundamental requirements of the genre of the ghazal to the highest degree.

Notes

1. 'Abbādī, *at-Tasfiya*, p. 140 f.
2. Aḥmad Ghazālī, *Savāniḥ*, p. 5.
3. E.g. the poem by Ḥāfiẓ cited below, in which the recurring verb *dāsht* ('he or she had, held, possessed') constitutes a *radīf* rhyme.
4. 'Oriental Pearls at Random strung', *Bulletin of the School of Oriental and African Studies*, Vol. xi, p. 699–712.
5. Cf. Franklin D. Lewis, *Reading, writing and recitation: Sanā'i and the origins of the Persian ghazal*, Chicago 1995 (privately published thesis).
6. For the use of these three terms to define to the Beloved in a ghazal, see A. Bausani in EI, s.v. G̲hazal ii.
7. B. Reinert, Enc.Ir., s.v. 'Aṭṭār.
8. 'Philologika XV. Farīduddīn 'Aṭṭār. III. 7. Der Dīwān.' in *Oriens* 12, 1959, pp. 1–88.
9. On the basis of his collected sermons, the *Ma'ārif*, Fritz Meier wrote a monumental study on his life and mystical ideas, *Bahā'-i Walad. Grundzüge seines Lebens und seiner Mystik*, Leiden 1989.
10. R. A. Nicholson, *Selected poems*, p. 107.
11. See on the imagery in Rūmī's lyrical poems in particular A. Schimmel, *The Triumphal Sun*.
12. See further Arberry, CPL, pp. 263–72.
13. J.D. Yohannan, *The poet Sa'dī*, New York 1987; R. Davis, EI, s.v. Sa'dī.
14. Rypka, HIL, p. 252.
15. P. Hardy, EI, s.v. Amīr Khusraw.
16. EI Suppl., s.v. 'Imād al-Dīn, Faḳīh-i Kirmānī; his ghazals were

studied by K. Stolz, in *Wiener Zeitschrift für die Kunde des Morgenlandes*, xlix, 1942, pp. 31–70.
17. Browne, LHP, iii, pp. 222–9; Arberry, CPL, pp. 316–19; Rypka, pp. 260–61.
18. G.M. Wickens, EI, s.v. Ḥāfiẓ; Michael C. Hillmann, *Unity in the Ghazals of Hafez*, Minneapolis and Chicago 1976; Michael Glünz and J. Christoph Bürgel (edd.), *Earthly and Heavenly. Seven Studies on the Poet Ḥāfiẓ of Shiraz*, Bern 1991; and the general works mentioned in the Bibliography.
19. See Browne, LHP, iii, p. 320–30, with specimens of his ghazals.
20. Browne, LHP, iii, pp. 333–44; Arberry, CPL, pp. 408–09.
21. Browne, LHP, iii, pp. 463–73; Arberry, CPL, pp. 412–17.
22. Browne, LHP, iii, pp. 473–87; Arberry, CPL, pp. 417–20.
23. Browne, LHP, iii, pp. 507–48; Arberry, CPL, pp. 425–49.
24. Browne, LHP, iv, pp. 229–30.
25. Browne, LHP, iv, pp. 265–76; Munibur Rahman, EI, s.v. Ṣā'ib.
26. EI, s.v. Shahriyār.
27. *Qābūs-nāma*, p. 195.
28. See in particular: Julie Meisami, *Medieval Persian Court Poetry*, Princeton 1987, Chapter VI, pp. 237–98: 'Ghazal: The Ideals of Love'.
29. A. Schimmel, *As Through a Veil*, pp. 11–48.
30. Summary of the discussion on *samā'* by Muḥammad Ghazālī, *Kīmiyā-yi sa'ādat*, pp. 369 ff.
31. On the use of erotic motives in homilies and its critics see De Bruijn, *Of Piety and Poetry*, pp. 164–70.
32. Leonard Lewisohn, *Beyond Faith and Infidelity. The Sufi Poetry of Mahmud Shabistari*, London 1995; EI, s.v. Maḥmūd Shabistarī.
33. Transl. R.A. Nicholson, *The Kashf al-maḥjúb. The oldest Persian treatise on Sufism*, p. 67.
34. Antinomian mysticism as a social phenomenon in the later Middle Ages is studied in Ahmet T. Karamustafa, *God's Unruly Friends: Dervish Groups in the Islamic Later Middle Period 1200–1550*, Salt Lake City 1994.
35. This passage in Suhrawardī's work was translated into German by H.Ritter, *Oriens* 12 (1959), pp. 14–16; see also the same, *Das Meer der Seele*, pp. 487–91.
36. The dervishes who followed the teachings of Jamāl ad-Dīn Sāvī (d. ab. 1232) were called *qalandars* in the hagiography that Khaṭīb Fārisī wrote more than a century later, at a time when the use of the term to denote antinomian practices was well established; see Karamustafa, Op.cit., pp. 39–44, and below Chapter 4, p. 119.
37. Several examples are given in an *excursus* on *qalandarīyāt* by

F. Meier, *Abū Sa'īd*, pp. 494–516; see also J.T.P. de Bruijn, 'The *Qalandariyyāt* in Persian mystical poetry, from Sanā'ī onwards', in L. Lewisohn (ed.), *Legacy*, pp. 75–86.

38. *Savāniḥ*, p. 12.
39. *Asrār at-tauḥīd*, i, p. 73.
40. Originally this ritual was ascribed to another legendary king of Iran, Khusraw, as it is still the case in Firdausī's *Shāh-nāma*.
41. On the story of Sheikh Ṣan'ān see also Chapter 4, p. 103.
42. Mentioned in Sūra ii, 25 ('Gardens underneath which rivers flow') and in many other places in the Koran.

4

Teachers and Story-tellers

The ma̱snavī

The distinction between lyrical and epic forms, familiar to the Western reader of poetry, is also often applied to Persian literature. Usually the meaning given to this pair of terms is more or less that of 'shorter' and 'longer' kinds of poetry. To the former belong the various types of poems we have discussed so far; in the latter category, there is only one form to be considered: the one which the Persians have named *ma̱snavī* using, as in the case of the *rubā'ī*, an Arabic term for a form of poetry which is highly characteristic of their own tradition.

The distinctive prosodical feature of the ma̱snavī is the internal rhyme of all distichs, which changes with each following line. The form is therefore comparable to an English poem in rhyming couplets. This relaxation of the strict mono-rhyme that was required for the lyrical forms made it possible to write long poems without ever being stopped by the exhaustion of rhymes. Although the origin of the ma̱snavī is not precisely known, the wish to enlarge the scope of their poems may very well have been a major incentive to the first Persian poets who opted for this particular pattern of rhyme. There certainly was a need for just such a form at the time when poets of the Islamic period began to use Persian for literary purposes. The Arabic conventions demanded a strict adherence to mono-rhyme, which virtually excluded the writing of long poems. The Persians, however, had inherited a rich tradition of narrative and didactical literature from their pre-Islamic past, which through this device could be incorporated in the classical poetry of the Islamic period where Arabic standards of prosody prevailed.

In contrast to Arabic literature, where poems in rhyming couplets remained a rarity, the Persians made abundant use of it from the very beginning. Already in the tenth century, poems of considerable length were written of which unfortunately no more than a few fragments survived. Rūdakī (d. 940), the most prominent poet at the court of the Samanids of Bukhara, wrote a version in ma̱snavī of the famous book of fables *Kalīla va Dimna*, based on the Sanskrit *Panchatantram*. Since the sixth century it was known in Persia in a Pahlavi translation, but Rūdakī probably used it in the Arabic version which was made in the ninth century by Ibn'l-Muqaffa', a key figure in the transmission of Pahlavi literature to the civilisation of Islam. The *Kalīla va Dimna* is more than just a collection of tales. It belongs to the genre of mirrors-for-princes, mostly exemplified in prose works, which give wise lessons on the ethics of kingship in an attractive form. The blending of the narrative and the didactical in Rūdakī's poem can also be detected in the remnants of Abū Shakūr's *Āfarīn-nāma* ('The Book of Praise', written in 948), who expounded secular wisdom with the addition of short anecdotes as illustrative asides.[1]

In addition, in later ma̱snavīs, the epic genre – in the sense of narrative poetry – is nearly always linked to the didactical. To many poets the moral advice hidden in their stories embodied the ultimate meaning of the poem, as did the explicit words of wisdom added to them. The greatest epic in Persian, Firdausī's *Shāh-nāma*, which was written about the year 1000, is a point in case. The long and varied tales of Iran's legendary history are in this poem tied to the author's wise and moralising excursions, which turn the ancient epic lore into an inexhaustible source of examples for kings and subjects alike. Conversely, the writer of a didactical ma̱snavī, who wanted to be first a moral teacher, equally needed the support of his alter-ego, the narrator. This fundamental trait of Persian narrative and didactical poetry had a great influence on the development of specifically mystical poetry in the ma̱snavī. One of its effects was that many of the great works written by mystical poets are at the same time masterpieces of narrative art; another, that many of these poems are far more accessible to modern readers than the lyrical forms usually are.

Didactical poetry

If one could characterise the Persian literary genius by a single pervasive trait, the tendency to moralising would be a good choice. This is easily supported by evidence from all periods, including both the pre-Islamic past and the modern literature of the twentieth century. In Zoroastrian literature, written in Pahlavi or Middle Persian, several *andarz-nāmag*s and *pand-nāmag*s, containing collections of wise sayings are known. What is being taught in this gnomic literature is *khirad*, 'wisdom'; this is a rather vague term referring to moral advice bearing on secular matters, although in the end the foundation of such advice was undoubtedly religious. In Islamic times, the Arabic term *ḥikmat* came into use for the same concept. Several Persian poets who became renowned for their wisdom were honoured with the epithet *ḥakīm*, the 'sage'. The kind of moralising comment given by the early poets just mentioned is of the same kind. As the religious notions expressed are of a most general kind, they do not provide the teaching of wisdom with a particular denominational colouring, be it Zoroastrian or Islamic.

It is necessary to mention this 'wisdom literature' as it is the most likely root from which mystical didactical poetry grew up. At the same time, it is helpful to make clear how tenuous the line is which divides secular from religious moralism. A useful criterium to make such a distinction might be the answer to the question whether or not the didactical work concerned has already a discernible Islamic colour by which it is distinguished from the more worldly type of wisdom. If we apply this criterium, we must conclude that there is no trace of any work that meets this standard before the middle of the eleventh century. The very first to be considered are two short ma<u>s</u>navīs, *Raushanā'ī-nāma* ('The Book of Illumination') and *Sa'ādat-nāma* ('The Book of Happiness'), which are handed down in manuscripts as works of Nāṣir-i Khusrau (1004 – ca.1075) whom we met earlier as a writer of didactical *qaṣīdas* and a propagandist of the Ismā'īlī Shi'a. The latter attribution is probably false, but the former poem is usually accepted as a genuine work. The *Raushanā'ī-nāma* would then be the first didactical poem with a distinct Islamic character still extant in its complete form. Yet, most of its contents are matters pertaining to life in the present world, discussed within the framework of religious ideas. The aim of the author is to outline the ideal way of life to be followed in anticipation of the life to come. For that reason he sketches the structure of the universe according to the order of creation, determining the position of man at the top of a pyramid of created beings, and concluding with the prospect of the Resurrection at the end of time. From here on Nāṣir continues to expound how man should prepare himself for a blissful existence in the afterlife.[2]

Nāṣir-i Khusrau cannot be considered as a Sufi poet by any definition. It may be assumed that, also in this little work, his main concern was the spread of Ismā'īlī doctrines. Yet, there is probably no statement to be found in this poem which would not be acceptable to Sufi readers who would abhor the thought of any affiliation with heterodox ideas. The link between cosmology on the one hand and the moral education of human beings on the other hand, established within the perspective of eternal salvation, is common to the entire tradition of didacticism by Sufi poets.

The beginnings of this tradition can be dated in the early decades of the twelfth century. Beginning in the first few decades of that century with Sanā'ī's contribution, a continuing line of works manifested itself, which rightly may be called a coherent tradition. These works are all unmistakably Islamic in outlook and were written with a mystical aim rather than an orientation towards the present world only. Those who participated in the tradition acknowledged the works of their predecessors and tried to emulate their example in one way or the other. Within the tradition a number of works stand out in particular as being the most influential models. The tradition of didactical poetry is an exceptionally long and rich one. It produced a great variety of works, but their connection with the mainstream of the tradition is usually evident.

The mas̲navīs of Sanā'ī

As we saw earlier, the life of Sanā'ī is closely interwoven with his literary work, and this is particularly true of his mas̲navīs. From the three poems he wrote in this form, two should be discussed here (the third, the *Kārnāma-yi Balkhī*, being an entirely secular work); both are dedicated to people who played an important and perhaps decisive role at a certain stage of his life. The first one is a very short poem, of nearly 750 distichs, and a sizeable section of it is of little interest to us because it contains merely a panegyric on the poet's patron, the chief *qadi* of the city of Sarakhs, Sayf ad-Dīn Muḥammad ibn Manṣūr. Its long Arabic title, *Sayr al-'ibād ilā'l-ma'ād* ('The Journey of the Servants to the Place of Return') is more telling than Persian book titles usually are, because it contains two allusions to phrases of the Koran which cannot have escaped the poem's readers.

The first allusion recalls the opening of the verse 'He made His servant travel in the night . . .' (Sūra xvii,1: *asrā bi-'abdih laylan* . . .), which the commentators of the Koran have taken to be a reference to the *mi'rāj*, the Prophet's Ascension to Heaven. This is, to the Islamic believer, not only the greatest event in the life of Muḥammad but also a powerful symbol of the highest goal to be reached by any human being. The journey goes upwards through the universe as it was conceived by medieval science, that is, the Ptolemaean system of the heavenly spheres which encloses the earth, and leads to an empyrean realm where spiritual beings dwell not burdened any longer by corruptible matter. Hardly a better parallel could be found for the course which human beings should follow in their efforts to free themselves from the bondage of this world. Persian poets have understood the force of this symbolism and have used it as a means to provide a deeper meaning to stories which on the surface might look quite mundane.

The word *ma'ād* of the title occurs only once in the Koran: 'He Who imposed the recitation upon thee shall surely restore thee to a place of homing' (Sūra xxviii, 85: *inna'llādhī faraḍa 'alayka'l-qur'āna la-rāddukum ilā ma'ādin*). Different explanations were suggested in the commentaries, but in the end the interpretation in an eschatological sense has prevailed. The 'last things' were a controversial topic in medieval Islam. Among philosophers it was held that after death the human being would return to its original spiritual state. The purpose of life was to make oneself ready for this eternal destination through moral purification and the acquisition of knowledge about the true nature of the created world. According to this theory, life is to be conceived as a cyclical process which offers humans the opportunity to perfect their pre-eternal souls. This doctrine was associated with the word *ma'ād* in the writings of the gnostics who are known as the 'Brethren of Purity' and who lived in Basra during the ninth century; it is also a key-term in the eschatological views of the greatest philosopher of the Muslim Middle Ages, Ibn-i Sīnā (d. 1037), or Avicenna as he is generally known in the West. The orthodox theologians of Islam attached different ideas to *ma'ād*. The idea of a separation between body and soul in the afterlife was unacceptable to them because it contradicted the dogma of the resurrection of the dead held to be one of the foundations of Islamic orthodoxy. In their view *ma'ād* could only mean the return of the souls to their resurrected bodies, which shall take place on the Day of Judgement.

This division of the minds on such an essential point of doctrine put a dilemma before Sufi writers. On the one hand, the philosophical concept of a cyclical development was an attractive model to them in order to describe the course of the mystical quest for unity. The ascetic training, consisting of gaining control over the forces emanating from the vegetative and the animal souls, was very much akin to the search for a liberation from physical existence as it had been preached over the centuries by gnostics and philosophers. The emphasis on the necessity of metaphysical knowledge as a means of salvation was equally congenial with Sufi thinking. On the other hand, it should not be overlooked that most Sufis were pious Muslims who could not entirely disregard the objections to the philosophical view on the destination of man on the part of orthodox theology.

In Sanā'ī's poem the two motifs of his title provide the key to a tightly phrased and often obscure allegory. The opening lines are adressed to 'the wind', a common device in Persian poetry to symbolise the idea of a message. The contents of this message is what he calls the 'vision' of his own 'creation'. The poet relates how, from the moment of the conception onwards, he travelled on towards the spiritual maturity necessary to recognise the perfect form after which he should strive in his lifetime. At the end of his journey he encounters his own model to be followed in the person of his patron, the high judge of Sarakhs. The story can be read, therefore, as a very personal account told in the first person and related to a specific time and place. It is obvious, however, that the poem also has a general significance, which makes it of particular interest as one of the oldest specimens of a didactical maṡnavī. One of the interesting features of the poem is that the stages of the journey are outlined simultaneously along a double track. The narrator traces, on the one hand, the successive stages of natural life, such as the embryonic stage, birth, physical development and the awakening of the human mind. Along this path he is guided by three personifications of the division of the human soul according to medieval psychology: before his birth by a nurse who represents the vegetative soul, in charge of the growth of the body; during the development of his lower spirit by a tyrant king symbolising the animal soul; and finally by a venerable and illuminated old man who represents the Active Intelligence, the intermediary between Universal Reason and the human intellect according to medieval philosophy.[3] In the following lines the old man describes his position in the cosmos:

He said: 'I am superior by nature and in rank;
My father is the Caretaker of God.

He was the first to come forth from eternity;
He is the sun who rose from non-existence.
The cause of this abode, of this creation;
Reflection of He sat down upon the Throne,[4]
He goes on weaving for your sake a garment
That will endure in spite of all decay.
On his command I stayed behind so long
Among this dust, in this polluted air.
For a good aim, not out of ignorance,
I stay as prisoner in an alien world.
Or else, would it be fitting:
A king's son as the guardian of dogs?
Would it not hurt one's pride:
A Gabriel among a swarm of flies?
I ask you! It cannot be that on this course
A fine horse shares the stable with the dogs.'[5]

Then the narrator and his guide travel through landscapes which form a replica of the universe. First, the itinerary goes through the sub-lunar world, where he meets with allegories of the forces of his lower soul, then through the heavenly spheres, each of which characterise a separate group of people who imperfectly cultivate their spiritual life, and finally it reaches the empyrean realm of the Universals, the place where the narrator finds his proper destination.

The reason for giving so much attention to this tiny poem is that it contains within a small compass a few of the essential themes of the entire tradition of the Sufi didactical poem. Notwithstanding its allegorical form, Sanā'ī's *Sayr al-'ibād* shows remarkable similarities to Nāṣir-i Khusrau's *Raushanā'ī-nāma*. In both texts, the structure of the universe as it was accepted as scientific truth in the age of the poet has been used as a background for a doctrine of salvation through the purification of the soul. Both writers connect their exposition to the expectation of a future life. The debate of the philosophers and the theologians on the proper meaning to be attached to this final goal of earthly existence is of little concern to the homiletic intention of their message. The importance to our present discussion is that this analysis has brought to light a fundamental structure of most of the works we are going to examine.

Sanā'ī's second maṯnavī differs in almost every aspect from the first one. On first sight, the only features the two works seem to have in common is that they both carry a long Arabic title and that they contain a fairly extensive panegyrical section. The poem is best known as *Ḥadīqat al-ḥaqīqa va-sharī'at aṭ-ṭarīqa*, 'The Garden of Reality and the Law of the Path', but in early manuscripts the alternative titles *Fakhrī-nāma* and *Ilāhī-nāma* are given to it as well. The former perhaps refers to one of the epithets of Bahrāmshāh, the Sultan of Ghazna to whom the maṯnavī was dedicated; the latter means 'Divine Book', an title often applied to religious works, for instance to one the poems of 'Aṭṭār which we will later discuss. It is possible that these different titles originally were related to different versions of the poem. One of the great problems of the *Ḥadīqa* is that, from the very beginning, it has been transmitted in various versions. There are indications that the poet died before he could give his poem its final form and it is impossible to reconstruct what he intended this to be. Even in the earliest manuscripts known to us, the size of the poem varies between 5,000 and 10,000 distichs which are in each case arranged in a quite different order. These philological problems are enhanced by the nature of the poem itself. It is not, like the *Sayr al-'ibād,* an allegory but a long drawn-out sermon, the coherence of which is often hard to detect. There are, however, compensations which make it understandable as to why this last work of Sanā'ī could achieve such great success, not only with his contemporaries but also among later generations in all countries where Persian books were read. The poem, with all its apparent chaos, deals in terse formulations with an immense variety of themes related to religion and morality. All this is illustrated by a wealth of images, brief tales and learned allusions. This has earned the poem the reputation of an 'Encyclopaedia of Sufism', but such an appellation can easily be misunderstood. Whatever uncertainties there may be concerning Sanā'ī's ultimate purpose, it is beyond any doubt that he never intended to write anything remotely like a systematic work. His real intent is quite conforming to his style: he delivers a homily to which all the manifold references to the outside world, to scientific knowledge or philosophical ideas are nothing but means used to make the homily compel the attention of the reader.

On the basis of the oldest version of the poem still extant (in a manuscript copied in 1157[6]) the following outline of Sanā'ī's original design may be given.

An introductory section discusses the general aspects of religious life, in particular man's obligations to his Creator, and the urgency to wake up from the 'slumber of neglectfulness' and prepare oneself for the eternal destination. The central significance of the Koran to the life of the soul and the example of a pious life given by the greatest men in the history of Islam are pointed out: not only the Prophet and the four 'rightly-guided' Caliphs Abū Bakr, 'Umar, 'Uthmān and 'Alī are included among them, but also 'Alī's sons Ḥasan and Ḥusayn (martyred Imams in the eyes of the Shi'ites) and al-Shāfi'ī and Abū Ḥanīfa, the founders of two of the schools of Sunnite law. Sanā'ī emphatically denies that there could be any contradiction between the pious reverence he paid to the 'People of the House' and his adherence to Sunni Islam. The doctrine of salvation he wants to expound implies more than Muslim piety alone: he also has much to say about the need for gnostic knowledge of the metaphysical structure of the universe and the constitution of the human psyche.

The transition to the second part is made through the introduction of a very brief allegory: the poet tells about his meeting with a spiritual Guide who represents the Intellect, a personification akin to the one appearing in the *Sayr al-'ibād ilā'l-ma'ād*. The homily then goes on to deal with the particular demands made on those who follow the path outlined by Sanā'ī. He talks extensively on matters of everyday life, including many subjects which seem to be directly relevant to his personal situation: sexual morality, the ethics of the profession of poetry, the equal rights of the Persian and Arabic languages as far as religion is concerned, old age and death, family life and the proper rules for eating, speaking and laughing. There is no apparent order in this catalogue of prescriptions, except for the repeated warnings to heed the powers of the lower soul which stimulate man to give in to the classical vices of lust, greed, aggression and jealousy, Sanā'ī's repeated condemnations of this world and his warnings of the approaching death. Finally, the ultimate goal is alluded to by a description of vernal nature symbolising the state of a purified human. This seemingly random sequence of themes reveals itself in the end as the stages of a 'Pilgrim's Progress'.

At this point another transition is made which brings the reader back to the reality of Sanā'ī's days. He starts to praise the Sultan of Ghazna, implying with panegyrical exaggeration that Bahrāmshāh embodies the perfect Islamic ruler. Very soon the discourse turns to ethical subjects again when he exposes the ethics of the ideal Islamic ruler, broaching themes familiar from works of the mirror-for-princes tradition. The poems ends with a lengthy plea by the poet to be excused from a close connection with the court because of his determination to spend the rest of his days in seclusion.

Sanā'ī's position as a pioneer of the Sufi tradition of didactical poetry is not without contradictions. As we have seen, both his short and his long poem cannot be detached entirely from the environment of their origin. In each case the teaching of the poet is, at least on the surface, directed to a man whom he wanted to honour as a model of human perfection, but with whom he also entertained a quite mundane relationship. Moreover, neither could be called a Sufi Master, not even Muḥammad ibn Manṣūr, although as a religious scholar and preacher he may very well have been a spiritual guide to the poet as well as a social protector.

These problems concerning the relationship between Sanā'ī's actual life and his work very soon lost their importance to posterity. What it inherited was a huge corpus of poetic formulations, contained in his poems, of themes pertaining to a wide range of religious and moral ideas. These were of the highest interest to poets and mystics alike. The first traces of Sanā'ī's impact are to be found already in the course of the twelfth century. Some poets actually claimed to be his successors in the style Sanā'ī had initiated. Khāqānī (1127–99), whom we mentioned earlier as one of the greatest Persian poets of the *qaṣīda*, prided himself as being 'a second Sanā'ī'. He wrote one ma̱snavī, the *Tuḥfat al-'Irāqayn* ('The Present from the Two Iraqs') in about 3,000 distichs.[7] This poem is concerned with a pilgrimage to Mecca, but primarily with a number of persons who were actual or prospective patrons of the poet. Although it should, for that reason, be characterised as a panegyric in the first place, it also contains several passages which show similarities to Sanā'ī's poems, such as the account of an allegorical journey through a country called *Quhistān*, ('Mountain Area'), the encounter with the guiding Intellect (in this case personified in the mythical figure of Khiẕr), and a lengthy praise of the Prophet including a description of the Ascension to Heaven. However, these elements do not allow us to classify this work in the category which concerns us here without reservation.

A mystical allegory comparable to Sanā'ī's *Sayr al-'ibād* is *Misbāh al-arvāḥ* ('Lantern of the Spirits'). This short ma̱snavī of about 1,100 distichs was written in a Sufi environment as it contains explicit references to the life in a mystical convent and the role of the *pīr*, or sheikh, as the leader of a Sufi order. The most likely author of the poem was Shams ad-Dīn Muḥammad ibn Īl-Ṭughān Bardasīrī. He probably lived slightly earlier than the well-known Sufi sheikh and poet Auḥad ad-Dīn Kirmānī (d. 1238) to whom the poem has been wrongly ascribed. The story is based on a pattern which, even more than that of Sanā'ī's poem, resembles the philosophical allegory *Ḥayy ibn Yaqẓān* ('The Living, son of the Vigilant') in Arabic prose which Avicenna wrote in the eleventh century. Climbing a mountain in the company of a group of intoxicated mystics the poet-narrator meets with a *pīr*. During a session of song and dance the Master starts to answer questions put to him by the narrator on 'the secret of creation' (*sirr-i āfarīnish*). The ensuing sermon by the *pīr* culminates in the exhortation to depart on a journey from 'Kirmān' to 'Egypt', meaning an itinerary leading from the material to the spiritual world. The successive landscapes the travellers pass through represent stations of the developing soul. The highest stage is called the *nafs-i fāniya*, the 'annihilated soul';

it is reached after the narrator has experienced a vision of the Prophet Muḥammad.[8]

The late twelfth century was also the period of a considerable expansion of mystical literature in prose. In addition, in these works the influence of Sanā'ī's didactical poetry is in evidence. A most remarkable example occurs in *'Abhar al-'āshiqīn* ('The Narcissus [or: Jasmine] of the Lovers'), a Persian treatise on mystical love by Rūzbihān-i Baqlī (1128–1209), one of the great mystics of Shiraz.[9] The theoretical exposition given in this work is introduced by an allegorical account of the poet's encounter with a personification of the Beloved during the visionary experience of a journey to the higher worlds. In the ensuing conversation verses drawn from Sanā'ī's *Ḥadīqat al-ḥaqīqa* are used by both partners, for instance in this brief dialogue:

I said: 'My dearest, from where did this beauty of yours come to me? Will you not tell me?'
He said: 'I was shaped by the hand of Divinity, to be a leader and a guide to Humanity.
The first thing created in this world was I, showing my face in every place.
All that was base and ugly I destroyed; my nature stayed aloof from all that was created.
God's eyes rest on me amongst all his creatures; for that I am unique in the created world.[10]

From the sixteenth century onwards the manuscripts of Sanā'ī's works contain other masnavīs as well, all of which have been proven to be written by others who happened to use the same metre *khafīf* of the authentic poems. The most extensive is *Ṭarīq al-taḥqīq* ('The Way of Establishing Truth'), which is now attributed to a Sufi named Aḥmad an-Nakhchavānī, who perhaps lived in the fourteenth century.[11] An interesting poem is also *'Ishq-nāma*, a poetical commentary of Aḥmad Ghazālī's *Savāniḥ*, which is now considered to have been written by the Sufi writer 'Izz ad-Dīn Maḥmūd Kāshānī (d. 1335), best known as one of the commentators of Ibn al-'Arabī's works.

Niẓāmī's Makhzan al-asrār

The first poet who frankly acknowledged his indebtedness to Sanā'ī as a writer of a didactical ma̱snavī was Ilyās ibn Yūsuf Niẓāmī of Ganja (1141–1209). He claimed that he could surpass his predecessor in a didactical poem, *Makhzan al-asrār* ('Treasury of Secrets'), a ma̱snavī of moderate size (about 2,250 distichs) for which he chose another metre, the *sarī'*, than Sanā'ī had used. The rather trivial reason of this literary rivalry was that Niẓāmī dedicated his work to another Bahrāmshāh, a semi-independent ruler of Erzincan in Eastern Anatolia. In this case, however, the panegyric is of little importance. Just as in the *Ḥadīqa*, the discourse is a continuous sermon, but Niẓāmī made a very clear plan for his poem. It is divided into twenty chapters, called *maqālas*, each with the same structure: first, a theoretical part, then an exemplary story and finally a conclusion attached to the story. Each chapter closes with an apostrophe to the poet himself containing his pen name just as this is done in the final line of a *ghazal*. Several of the stories in the *Makhzan al-asrār* have become well known; for example the Saljuq Sultan Sanjar hearing the advice of a poor old woman, King Nūshirvān and his minister listening to the conversation of two birds in a ruined village, and Jesus explaining to his disciples the meaning of the shining teeth of a dead dog.

The contents of Niẓāmi's poem are indicated in the headings added to each chapter. It should, however, be considered that it is written in the typically homiletic style which also characterises its model. Usually the poet soon strays away from the subject he started with so that it is often difficult to follow the meandering line of his thoughts and exhortations. The general message of the discourse cannot be missed, however. Niẓāmī preaches on the ideal way of life drawing the attention of his reader to the supreme rank of man among the creatures of this world, the approaching end of his life and the necessity to become aware of his eternal destination. In a few chapters he speaks more specifically about the duties of a king, but on the whole he addresses himself to mankind in general rather than to his royal patron.

A special feature of the poem is the extensive introduction which contains the account of the experiences the poet claims to have had during his solitary vigils, called *khalvat*. There is no indication that one should take these vigils to the letter, that is as the report of actual Sufi practices. They really are nothing but a literary fantasy used by Niẓāmī to expose his ideas on the duties of the spiritually inclined poet he wanted to be. The aim he pursues in this work is to transcend the limitations of the secular literature of the courts. In a mannered and highly rhetorical style he relates the allegory of a search for his own heart. With this Niẓāmi joins in a discussion on the destination of Persian poetry which had started with Sanā'ī and was continued by others, in the first place by 'Aṭṭār.[12]

After this early didactical work, Niẓāmī turned to narrative poetry. His four other ma<u>s</u>navīs are together with the *Makhzan al-asrār* known as the *Khamsa*, the 'Five Poems'. One of these, *Majnūn and Layla*, tells about the self-denying love of the 'possessed' (*majnūn*) Arabic poet Qays for a girl from another bedouin tribe, which became a favourite example for mystical poetry. In an inserted admonition, Niẓāmī emphasises that the story could be read as a parable of mystical love as well as a tale of earthly love.[13] The remaining poems – *Haft Paykar*, 'The Seven Images', *Khusrau and Shīrīn*, and *Iskandar-nāma* ('The Book of Alexander') – deal with subjects related to the epic history of Iran. It is a difficult to decide whether or not these masterpieces of Persian narrative poetry should be dealt with in this survey. On the surface, they are typical products of the secular literature of the courts, the mentality of which they faithfully reflect. Even if Niẓāmī frequently gives in to moralising and wise reflections, overt formulations of mystical ideas are rare and, moreover, mostly restricted to the introductions of the poems where the literary convention prescribed the treatment of religious themes like the praise of God and the Prophet. The prominence given to descriptions of Muḥammad's Ascension to Heaven in these introductions undoubtedly suggests the possibility of an alternative, symbolic reading of these tales about frantic poets, amorous kings and conquerors of the world. This certainly conforms with the lofty concept of the poet's calling so strongly expressed in Niẓāmī's first work. However, a one-sided esoterical reading of these romances would be mistaken as it would ignore the basic duality of meaning which is such a fascinating feature of Niẓāmī's art.[14]

The masnavī's of 'Aṭṭār

Farīd ad-Dīn 'Aṭṭār was probably a slightly younger contemporary of Niẓāmī's. It is unknown whether the two poets, who spent their apparently uneventful lives in different parts of Persia, knew about each other's works. However, they do have at least two things in common: they made important contributions to the tradition of the mystical masnavī, and they were both great story-tellers. Of one of 'Aṭṭār's poems it could even be said that it resembles the romantic stories of Niẓāmī: the *Khusrau-nāma* tells about the adventures of a fictitious pair of lovers, without giving any clue to a mystical connotation. The other works of 'Aṭṭār, however, are purely mystical works in which narration plays a major role as a means to conveying the theoretical concepts in the more accessible form of a parable.

There is, however, a problem of another kind facing the student of 'Aṭṭār's works. If we were to believe the evidence of the attributions occurring in most manuscripts, 'Aṭṭār would have been an exceptionally prolific writer of didactical masnavīs. The complete list comprises about twenty titles. Serious doubts about the authenticity of several of these works were voiced for the first time by the Persian scholar Sa'īd Nafīsī in 1941. He was able to trace a number of them to another poet who also names himself 'Aṭṭār, but actually lived in the second of the fifteenth century, that is two-and-a-half centuries later than Farīd ad-Dīn, the pharmacist of Nishapur. Moreover, this other 'Aṭṭār reveals himself to be a fervent Shi'ite, whereas his older namesake left no doubt about his adherence to the tenets of the Sunni majority. The odd thing is that the fifteenth century author occasionally poses as if he really were Farīd ad-Dīn 'Aṭṭār. We must therefore conclude that this is not a case of wrong attribution, but of deliberate mystification.[15]

Apart from these notoriously unauthentic poems, the list of ʻAṭṭār's works also contains a few titles the true authorship of which has been put into doubt by modern scholars mainly on stylistic grounds. The most important of the latter is *Ushtur-nāma,* 'The Book of the Camel', an extensive ma̱snavī in two parts relating the quest of mystical travellers who are compared to camels in the caravan of the pilgrimage to Mecca. In the introduction of the poem the image of a Turkish puppet player who performs with seven curtains is used as a symbol of the Creator and the Universe.[16] In all the works of this group, to which also *Bīsar-nāma* ('The Book of the Beheaded') and *Haylāj-nāma*[17] belong, the poet's devotion to the mystical martyr Manṣūr al-Ḥallāj is a central theme.

The group which is unquestionably authentic consists mainly of four poems of more or less equal length. These four were chosen by the German scholar Hellmut Ritter as the sources for his monumental study on ʻAṭṭār, *Das Meer der Seele. Mensch, Welt und Gott in den Geschichten des Farīduddīn ʻAṭṭār* ('The Ocean of the Soul. Man, World and God in the stories of Fariduddin ʻAṭṭār'). As the title indicates, Ritter based his analysis on the narratives to be found in these poems. From the wealth of references contained especially in the shorter tales and anecdotes a masterful picture of the spirituality of a mystic of ʻAṭṭār's age is drawn.

ʻAṭṭār's great interest in narrative art is noticeable first of all in the use of the device of a frame story in three of these four poems. This device came to Persia from India in the late Sasanian period with the translation of collections of fables such as the *Kalīla va Dimna*. To Western readers it is familiar from the tale of Shehrazade's story-telling, which binds together the collection of popular tales in the *Arabian Nights*. Stories of this kind were often rather sketchy, having little function besides providing the required coherence to the subject matter of a book of stories. ʻAṭṭār's choice of stories for this purpose was, however, much more sophisticated. In each case the encompassing tale is meaningful in its own right so that their summaries provide valuable indications about the poet's ideas.

To the general reader in the West, *Manṭiq aṭ-ṭayr* ('The Speech of the Birds', sometimes also called *Maqāmāt aṭ-ṭuyūr*, 'The Stages of the Birds') is by far the best known. This is due mainly to the nineteenth-century French translation by Garcin de Tassy, which was translated many times over into other Western languages.[18]

In the *Manṭiq aṭ-ṭayr*, the story of the frame work was taken from a symbolic tale about birds, which in the twelfth century had been told in Arabic and Persian prose respectively by Muḥammad and Aḥmad Ghazālī. The use of the bird as a symbol of the human soul, implied in that story, is even attested earlier in philosophical allegories among the writings of Ibn Sīnā (d. 1037) in Arabic poetry and prose. In 'Aṭṭār's poem, the plot turns essentially on the search for the perfect representative of a category of beings, be it birds or humans. One day, the birds gather to discuss the choice of a king under whose authority they could unite in spite of all their differences. The lead is taken by the hoopoe (*hudhud*), who reveals that the real 'Sultan of the birds' is the miraculous bird Sīmurgh nestling at the end of the world. The birds are thrilled by his description of the glory of this sovereign and ask the hoopoe how the journey to the Sīmurgh's court could be made. Then a voice is heard warning them of the mortal dangers of this quest, and one after another the birds excuse themselves from such a perilous enterprise. In the end, only a small group sets out under the guidance of the hoopoe. The journey leads them through a desert with seven valleys; their names betray what is meant by this itinerary: 'search', 'love', 'gnosis' (*ma'rifat*), 'being self-contained' (*istighnā*), 'confession of unity' (*tauḥīd*), 'bewilderment', and 'poverty'. The stages remind of the *manāzil*, the succession of states in the classical training of the Sufis, but there are significant differences. The process outlined by 'Aṭṭār has a meaning of its own, which is the gradual initiation to the Divine essence of the Sīmurgh and the preparation for the final encounter. The journey is extremely arduous and causes many casualties among the birds. Eventually, only thirty birds (in Persian *sī murgh*) reach the Sīmurgh; on the basis the popular etymology of the miraculous bird's name this amounts to finding their own essence. Even this is not the end of their plight because they are not admitted to the inaccessible court before they have laid down all illusions about themselves and the world, and have reached a state of absolute indigence. When in the end an audience is granted, the Sīmurgh teaches them that true salvation can only be reached in the afterlife. In anticipation of that blissful state they are urged to clean their souls, to pray to God and to remember His Name.

The story is full of allusions to motifs and images which were quite familiar to the educated reader of 'Aṭṭār's days. The very title of the poem was taken from the Koran (Sūra xxvii, 16), where Solomon boasts of his knowledge of the 'speech of the birds'. The hoopoe also belongs to the saga of Solomon, where he is the king's messenger to Bilqīs, the queen of Sheba. The seven valleys not only recall the stages of the Sufi path, but also the route through the Arabian desert to be followed on a pilgrimage to Mecca. Moreover, if imagined as going into a vertical direction, they correspond to the ascent through the Ptolemaean spheres which, as we have seen, was a standard analogy of the climb to a perfected state of being. The figure of Sīmurgh was borrowed from the ancient epic tradition of Persia.[19]

The other narratives in the poem are usually told by one of the characters of the frame story, especially by the hoopoe when he answers the questions of the other birds. Here as well as in the other poems 'Aṭṭār avails himself of the mass of stories current in medieval Islam. Being the author of a great collection of hagiographies of Sufi saints, *Taẕkirat al-auliyā*, he was well versed in that particular branch of narrative. Important are also stories about Muḥammad, his companions and the other prophets recognised by Islam. There are numerous other anecdotes and anonymous tales derived from written sources, from an oral tradition or perhaps invented by 'Aṭṭār himself.

One story stands out from all the others. First through its exceptional length: with more than 400 distichs it is almost a short maṯnavī by itself. It also serves as an important pivot in the structure of the poem; the hoopoe tells it when he is winding up of his argument and the birds are about to venture upon their search. Finally, it amply illustrates an idea expressed repeatedly by 'Aṭṭār: the demand for a radical elimination of the awareness of self. Essentially the same thought is preached by the Sīmurgh at the conclusion of the poem.

In the holy precinct of Mecca once lived a very famous Sufi Master by the name of Sheikh Ṣan'ān (in some early manuscripts of the *Manṭiq aṭ-ṭayr* he is called Sam'ān), a mystic whose historical identity is uncertain.[20] He is the revered teacher of four-hundred pupils, who all are already accomplished mystics themselves. One night he dreams of a very beautiful Christian girl, who lives in Byzantine Anatolia. The Sheikh cannot put her image out of his mind, and all of a sudden he leaves Mecca to seek her. When he finds the girl, she makes the fulfilment of his amorous wish dependent on a number of conditions, all of which signify the renunciation of Islam and all the Sheikh's pious principles. At the bottom of his descent into utter degradation, he becomes the girl's swineherd. In the meantime, a group of faithful adepts sets out to look for him. They find him in this wretched state. Their prayer for God's help is answered. The Sheikh has a vision of the Prophet Muḥammad and, after a vigil of forty days, he is freed from his obsession. He converts the girl to Islam just before she dies. To explain this strange adventure he reveals to the adepts that, in spite of his advanced mystical stage, a serious obstacle had remained on his path: the esteem in which he held his own piety. Such a trace of selfishness could only be removed by the experience of sin in its most abject form. This idea is identical to the antinomian ideas expressed in the *qalandarī* poetry discussed in the previous chapter.

The *Ilāhī-nāma* contains the story of a Caliph and his seven sons who are filled with high ambitions. One day the father asks each of them about his most cherished wishes. As it appears, the princes all have set their minds on something which belongs to the sphere of fairy tales and folklore: the princess of the Peris, the cup of the ancient king Jamshīd, the magic ring of Solomon, the elixir of the alchemist and so on. The Caliph fulfils each one of their wishes, as he had promised, but not in the way the sons had expected it. With the help of tales fitting his argument, he convinces his sons that their aspirations for sensual pleasure, power, riches and other values of this world should be turned into the strive for higher aims. They should learn to understand their desires as emblems of the successive stages along the path towards the mystical goal. There the body will be transformed through a spiritual alchemy into a heart, and this heart will be filled with the pain of mystical love. Beyond this, ʿAṭṭār concludes, there are more secrets, but the divulgence of these is only permitted on the gallows – a clear reference to the martyrdom of ʿAṭṭār's spiritual hero Manṣūr al-Ḥallāj. The allegorical meaning of this plot is explained right from the beginning: the Caliph personifies the human spirit; the six sons stand for the faculties and inclinations of the soul.

A straightforward allegory is also the *Muṣībat-nāma*, 'The Book of Affliction'. Introducing the poem, ʿAṭṭār explains how this poem should be read: as a story told in *zabān-i ḥāl*, the 'speech of condition'. Although the story would be false if it were judged by the rules of 'ordinary speech' (*zabān-i qāl*), it contains in fact the very truth. By way of an alternative he proposes to call the former 'speech of meditation' (*zabān-i fikrat*). The technique to which ʿAṭṭār refers consists of using various items, concrete as well as abstract, as emblems who explain their own special qualities in a symbolic manner.

The leading character is a mere allegorical shadow, the personification of meditation as a 'traveller' (*sālik*). The 'affliction' mentioned in the title of the poem could perhaps best be characterised as an 'existential crisis': the meditating subject travels around the universe in search of his identity as a human being. He is motivated by the observation of the world and its inhabitants, including mystics, Sufis and ascetics, who try in vain to find the right answers to their queries. In his deepest despair, Divine Help sends him a 'living *pīr*' who guides his quest for the truth about himself. The journey on which they set out comprises both outer and inner strata of the universe. There are forty stages – the number of the days and nights of a Sufi vigil. It is worthwhile to describe here the entire itinerary because also in this poem the frame story reveals much of the poet's intentions.

The journey follows a double track: first, a descent from the transcendental to the material world, and then an ascent which amounts to a return towards spiritual spheres of existence. This conforms to the view of human life in this world as a cycle. In each half of the cycle several sequences can be distinguished as follows:

A. *The descending curve:*
1. The realm of the archangels: Gabriel (the Messenger of God), Asrāfīl (the Angel of the Ressurrection), Michael (the Sustainer of Life) and 'Azrā'īl (The Angel of Death).
2. The transcendental entities which belong to traditional Islamic lore: God's Throne, the Platform (supporting the Throne), the Table of Destiny, the Pen of the Divine Decree, Paradise and Hell.
3. The astral heavens: the Firmament, the Sun and the Moon.
4. The elements and major forms of the lower world: Fire, Air, Water, Earth, the Mountains and the Sea.

B. *The ascending curve:*
1. The kingdoms of the lower world: Minerals, Plants, Wild Animals, Birds, Cattle, the Devil (Iblīs), Demons and Man.
2. The Prophets as they are recognised by Islam: Adam, Noah, Abraham, Moses, David, Jesus and Muḥammad.
3. The divisions of human psyche: the Senses, Imagination, Intellect, the Heart and the Soul (Rūḥ).

The traveller and his guide pay a visit to each item, which then provides the emblematic explanations proper to its nature. These are interpreted each time by the *pīr* at the hand of parables and anecdotes. The climax of the story is reached just before the last series of visits when they meet with the Prophet of Islam. Only Muḥammad is able to provide the right answer to the traveller's question by showing him that the way towards knowledge of the Divine passes through knowledge of one's own self.

The design of this allegory has been compared with the Islamic idea of the mediation between man and God assigned to the Prophet, which is expressed by the Arabic term *shafāʿa*. There is also some resemblance to the use of allegory by Sanāʾī in the *Sayr al-ʿibād ilāʾl-maʿād* as far as the figure of the guide and the metaphysical itinerary are concerned.

The proper chronology of ʿAṭṭār's works has not yet been established. There remain, for instance, conflicting opinions about the date of the *Asrār-nāma* ('The Book of Secrets'). According to Christiane Tortel, the French translator of this poem,[21] it would be the work of his old age, but Andrew Boyle considered it to be the first of the four mystical poems.[22] Whatever the case may be, an early dating of the poem would provide a better explanation for the fact that this is the only of ʿAṭṭār's four poems lacking a frame story. Although it is divided into chapters, it is written in the same homiletic form which was used earlier by Sanāʾī and Niẓāmī. This might be an argument in favour of the assumption that ʿAṭṭār wrote the *Asrār-nāma* before the narrative gained such an overwhelming importance in his didactical poetry.

In order to give an impression of the particular style of this poem we will examine here part of his discourse. The passage is taken from the beginning of the sixth chapter (the division into chapters is a rather arbitrary one; headings which could give a suggestion of the central idea dealt with in each case are lacking).

The poet starts to denounce the world for its delusive nature. However immense the world may appear to the eye, in reality it is not the sea itself but merely the froth on the surface; it is a fantasy, a ghost as a child might see in a piece of glass. The true source of the secrets dealt with in this poem should be sought far above this world, near the Throne of God. ʿAṭṭār adduces the example of the Arabic alphabet which is meaningless in itself. All the curves of the letters are merely a screen hiding their emptiness. One could learn this already from the first letter, the *alif*, which is written as a straight vertical line; moreover, the *alif* is the essential letter of the Arabic word *lā*, 'no'. This word his a special significance as it is the word opening the first part of the Muslim creed: 'There is no god but Allah.'

A new theme is introduced when the comment of a pious man on the *amānat*, 'the burden of trust', is cited. By this, reference is made to a verse in the Koran which was very popular with the Sufi poets: 'We offered the burden of trust to the Heavens and the Earth and the Mountains, but they refused to carry it and recoiled from it. Man has carried it. He is truly an ignorant sinner' (Sūra xxxiii, 72). The mystic in this short tale concludes from this verse that man, by accepting God's *amānat*, has forfeited his life.

On the one side there is the unworthiness of the world; on the other side the awesome task God has imposed on the human being in spite of all his shortcomings. This assignment, 'Aṭṭār continues, can only be fulfilled by those who are willing to 'lose their head'. By this the supreme act of self-denial is meant which in the tradition of Sufism is connected with the name of Ḥallāj.

A dream is related which shows Ḥallāj carrying both his severed head and a cup filled with rosewater. This, so he declares, is the cup of welcome bestowed by the 'King with the Good Name' on those who sacrificed their heads.

Only by forgetting about your own head, 'Aṭṭār explains, you may hope to be able to drink from the cup of 'meaning', which will transform all that was body into soul and thus enable you to loose yourself entirely in the 'Name'. (This turn of the discourse is made with the help of a pun on the Arabic words *jism*, 'body' and *ism*, 'name'.)

Another parable, illustrating the same point of 'Aṭṭār's argument, tells about a proud king who, passing by a road with all his pomp and circumstance, sees a poor man without any care in the world at the side of the road and asks him: 'Would you not rather be me?' The poor man replies: 'My deepest wish is to be not me.'

As this paraphrase of a passage of no more than thirty lines shows, the dense use of imagery, word-play and a few illustrative tales enables the didactical poet to express a connected line of profound mystical thoughts quite effectively within a very small compass. The great art of this homiletic style lies not so much in the attractiveness of the narratives, which are usually very short indeed, but in the flashing movement of the poet's discourse from one theme to another. It was this style as it is exemplified in the *Asrār-nāma* which characterised both the didactical poetry of ʻAṭṭār's predecessor Sanā'ī and that of his successor Maulānā Jalāl ad-Dīn Rūmī.

Rūmī's Masnavī-yi Maʻnavī

An ancient anecdote reports that Jalāl al-Dīn and his father Bahā ad-Dīn Valad visited the aged poet ʻAṭṭār in Nishapur when, about 1215, they journeyed from their native town Balkh, in the North of present-day Afghanistan, to the West. On that occasion ʻAṭṭār would have presented the young boy with a copy of his *Asrār-nāma*. Whether or not this is historical fact cannot be decided, but even if it is merely a product of pious fantasy, there is certainly an element of truth in the story as it confirms the indubitable fact of ʻAṭṭār's impact on Jalāl ad-Dīn's own contribution to the tradition of the didactical masnavī. None of the former's four mystical poems is more likely to have provided a model to the *Masnavī-yi maʻnavī* of the latter than the *Asrār-nāma* with its homiletic design.

There is another story relevant to the beginning of Jalāl ad-Dīn's work on his great poem. It is told in *Manāqib al-ʻārifīn* ('The Virtues of the Mystics') by Shams ad-Dīn Aḥmad Aflākī, a hagiographical account of the origins of the Mevlevi Order written in the fourteenth century.[23] Aflākī quotes a reciter of the *Masnavī* at the tomb of Maulānā at Konya, who told him that the brothers of the early community used to study the *Ilāhī-nāma* (i.e. Sanā'ī's *Ḥadīqat al-ḥaqīqa*) as well as ʻAṭṭār's *Manṭiq aṭ-tayr* and *Muṣībat-nāma* with great devotion, but found it difficult to understand the style of these works. Jalāl ad-Dīn's intimate of that moment, Ḥusām ad-Dīn, asked him to compose a similar work of his own, on the lines of Sanā'ī's poem and in the metre of the *Manṭiq aṭ-ṭayr*. In reply to this Jalāl ad-Dīn drew a sheet of paper from his turban and handed this to Ḥusām ad-Dīn. The first eighteen lines of the poem were written on it already in the requested metre.

As Aflākī continues, from then onwards the text of the poem was dictated to Ḥusām whenever Jalāl ad-Dīn felt inspired. This could happen during a mystical session, in a public bath or in any other circumstance. Afterwards the lines noted down were read out to Jalāl ad-Dīn and corrected by him. However, Ḥusām's part in the creation of the poem was much more than that of a humble scribe. He is repeatedly and emphatically named in the poem as the principal source of Jalāl ad-Dīn's inspiration, almost in the same manner as Sham ad-Dīn Tabrīzī was mentioned in Rūmī's *ghazals*. When Ḥusām was overwhelmed by grief because of the death of his wife, the work on the poem came to a stand-still for two years. At the beginning of the second book, it is mentioned that the writing was resumed in the year 662 AH (1263–64) (the date of the beginning of the work is unknown). The entire poem was completed shortly before Maulānā Rūmī's death in 1273.

The *Masnavī yi Ma'navī* is by far the greatest work in the tradition which we survey here, both in a literal and a figurative sense. The poem, of no less than 25,632 distichs (in R.A. Nicholson's edition), is divided into six books, each of which is preceded by a preface in ornate Arabic prose. The first book opens with the passage referred to in Aflākī's anecdote, dealing with the reed pipe. Many suggestions have been made for the interpretation of this motif. It has been taken as a symbol of either Ḥusām ad-Dīn or the poet himself, as the embodiment of abstract mystical concepts such as 'the soul of the Saint or Perfect Man' (Nicholson),[24] or, on the other hand, been related to the discussion on the use of music by mystics, which has always been very prominent in the ritual of the 'dancing dervishes' of the Mevlevi Order (Ahmed Ateş).[25]

Such overall readings of this motif do not do justice to its rhetorical function as the opening of a poem. Following an old tradition of Persian poetry, Jalāl ad-Dīn has resorted to the device of an emblematic prologue, on the same lines as Sanā'ī's opened his *Sayr al-'ibād* with an address to the wind. Taking – perhaps not by accident – the reed pipe as his theme he applied the same device of the 'speech of condition'(*zabān-i ḥāl*) on which 'Aṭṭār based his *Muṣībat-nāma*. If the prologue of the *Masnavī-yi ma'navī* is read carefully, the application of this technique reveals itself.

In the opening line the reader is exhorted to listen to the 'complaint' of the reed pipe which tells a tale of 'separations'. Then the reed pipe speaks:

Since I was cut off from the reed-land,
Men and women have lamented through my sound.
I want separation to pierce and pierce my breast
So that I may reveal the pain of my longing.
Whoever stays far away from his roots,
Tries to regain the time of conjunction.
My lament can be heard in every gathering;
I am with the distressed and the happy ones.
Whoever joined me with ideas of his own
Did not seek the secrets hidden inside me.
My secret is not far from my lament,
But to eye and ear it remains in the dark:
Body and soul are not veiled to each other
Yet no one is allowed to see the soul.[26]

Modern readers, especially in the West, have difficulty in finding any structure in Rūmī's poem. If its character as a didactical discourse, which continues over the entire length of the six books, is recognised, however, the coherence proper to the poem reveals itself quite clearly. By means of subtle associations, imaginative or conceptual, the poet twists the thread of his ideas. In spite of all the richness of its narrative contents, the *Ma<u>s</u>navī-yi ma'navī* is far from being a storybook. Rūmī is a very strange narrator indeed because he frequently seizes the first opportunity to deviate from the story he has just begun, in order to enter into a theoretical discussion which is often only associated with a minor detail of the story. Such excursions may present new occasions for a parable, so that a minor tale is told while the main story is kept waiting. Whoever is willing to follow Rūmī in the meanderings of his discourse, however, sees a fascinating panorama of mystical ideas unfolding. Some of the themes broached are related to the immediate concerns of the poet at the time of his dictation, as for instance when he lectures on the correct behaviour of his adepts and their religious education. Others develop subjects also dealt with in the works of Rūmī's predecessors, for example the development of the human being to his full perfection which is expounded in a manner reminiscent of Sanā'ī. The most intimate parts of the poem deal with Jalāl ad-Dīn Rūmī's very personal concept of Divine love.[27] Already quite early in the poem a passage is inserted where the poet seems to let himself be carried away by the image of the sun. What he actually does is to seek an opportunity to speak, however briefly, about Shams ad-Dīn, 'the Sun of Religion', the beloved friend from Tabriz over whose tragic disappearance he is still mourning. When he finally names him, his own soul intervenes entreating him to continue and to talk openly of Shams ad-Dīn. At this point the poet recoils from the awesome topic:

Should he appear to the naked eye, I said,
You could not endure it, not any part of you.
Wish what you may, but know the measure of your wish:
A blade of straw can never move a mountain.
The sun who gives his light to this world
Would scorch it if he came a little closer.
Do not seek discord, strife and bloodshed;
Do not talk any more about the Sun of Tabriz!'[28]

Sulṭān Valad

After the death of Maulānā Rūmī the leadership of the community in Konya was first taken over by Ḥusām ad-Dīn and then, in 1284, when the latter had also died, by Rūmī's eldest son Bahā ad-Dīn Muḥammad (1226–1312), better known as Sulṭān Valad. He was the founder of the Mevlevi Order which developed from the community of Rūmī's adepts. Until the early twentieth century, when it was officially abolished by the Turkish

Republic, the leadership of the Order remained in the hands of his descendants. Sulṭān Valad was trained as a religious scholar and a mystic, not only by his father, but also by his father's own teacher Burhān ad-Dīn Muḥaqqiq. Later he followed the guidance of Salāḥ ad-Dīn Farīdūn Zarkūb ('the Goldsmith'), one of the earliest biographers of Rūmī, to whose daughter Fāṭima he was married. The close bond with his father was expressed by the latter when he said to him: 'You are among all people the one who is most like me in character and physical appearance.' This was taken by Sulṭān Valad as an incentive to follow closely his father's example, including all his varied literary activities. He wrote *ghazal* poetry in the same vein, and produced a prose work, the *Ma'ārif*, dealing with Sufi topics similar to Rūmī's own collection of informal sermons, *Fīhi mā fihi*.

His most important works are three connected ma̱snavīs, the first of which, written in the summer of 1291, is usually named *Valad-nāma*, although the title *Ibtidā'ī-nāma* ('The Book of Beginning') has been applied to it as well. It is a long poem, of more than 8,000 distichs. Brief prose texts, written in a fairly simple style, alternate with the ma̱snavī lines, summarising the most important ideas which subsequently are developed in the poetic discourse. The choice of the metre *khafīf* shows a recognition of Sanā'ī, who is cited several times, but the poem is not a close imitation of the *Ḥadīqat al-ḥaqīqa*. Although much information is given on the lives of Rūmī and his close associates, the poem is not a hagiography in the usual sense. Sulṭān Valad's aim was to disclose the mystical truth represented by their lives, which in *Ma̱snavī-yi ma'navī* was hidden behind stories about prophets and saints who had lived in the past. The emphasis is not on the events for their own sake but on the mystical ideas they reveal. In fact, the *Valad-nāma* contains an invaluable statement of Rūmī's thought as it was understood by the first generation of his followers.

Like the poems of Sanā'ī and Rūmī, the *Valad-nāma* belongs to the homiletic type of ma̱snavī. The use of long stories, repeatedly interrupted by short anecdotes or theoretical asides and of a rich imagery, also follow the example of Rūmī. The unique relationship between Rūmī and Shams ad-Dīn is actually the first episode from Rūmī's life related in the poem. According to Sulṭān Valad the emotional experience of Shams' disappearance[29] changed his father from a devout Islamic scholar into a ecstatic poet of love:

The separation made a Majnūn of the Sheikh:
Love robbed him, like Dhū'n-Nūn,[30] *of head and feet.*
Love turned the pious Mufti into a poet:
He who was an ascetic began to sell wine.
Not wine as it is pressed from grapes:
This Soul of Light drank the wine of Light.[31]

Sulṭān Valad's other poems supplement the *Valad-nāma* by developing some of themes of that poem. One is known as *Rabāb-nāma* ('The Book of the Rebeck') because this instrument is used as an introductory emblem in the same manner as the flute in the prologue of Rūmī's maṯnavī. The third poem is simply entitled *Intihā'ī-nāma*. Sulṭān Valad wrote a few lines in Turkish, which some modern scholars have hailed as a first sign of an emerging Sufi poetry in Ottoman Turkish.

Sa'dī's Būstān

Another classic maṯnavī written in the thirteenth century is Sa'dī's *Būstān*, 'The Orchard'. He wrote the poem, so he tells, in 1257 as a present to the good people of Shiraz when he came home after a long period of travelling. It differs considerably from the works we have just discussed. The text is divided into ten clearly defined chapters. Within each chapter the stories are the most prominent part and many theoretical comments are put into the mouth of one of the characters. Besides, the *Būstān* belongs as much to court poetry as to the Sufi tradition. The work is dedicated to the local ruler of Shiraz, Abū Bakr ibn Sa'd-i Zangī, and the first two chapters constitute a mirror-for-princes, stressing the need for justice and good care of the subjects. The poem is written in the metre *mutaqārib* which, apart from the early didactical poem by

Abū Shakūr (tenth century), had been mostly reserved for secular epics, in the first place Firdausī's *Shāh-nāma*.

Yet it would be a mistake to separate the *Būstān* entirely from the tradition of Sufi poetry. Most of the material in the remaining chapters is concerned with the ethics of the moderate kind of mysticism Sa'dī adhered to. Although it is unknown whether he really belonged to any of the Sufi orders of his time, he refers to the great mystic Shihāb ad-Dīn Abū Ḥafṣ 'Umar as-Suhravardī in Baghdad (d. 1234) as his teacher and frequently associates himself with the way of life of the dervishes. The most profound statement of his mysticism is to be found in the third chapter, devoted to 'Love and drunkenness and ecstacy' (*dar 'ishq va mastī va shūrī*). In a sequence of more than twenty stories he exemplifies the rapture of the 'followers of the Path', their self-sacrifice and endurance of the sufferings they are afflicted with. The emotions experienced in the love for someone who is made of 'water and clay', which is based on lust, is no more than a remote analogy of the experience of those who 'forget their own soul (*jān*) yearning for the (divine) Beloved (*jānān*)'. Sa'dī concludes with the celebrated dialogue between the moth and the candle who compare their common misery caused by love. On a sleepless night, the poet overhears the moth asking the candle:

The lover, I am; it befits me to burn;
but what is the reason for your weeping and burning?
The candle replied: 'Oh my ill-fated lover,
a honey-sweet [shīrīn] *friend went away from me.*
Someone like Shīrīn has deserted me;
there is fire on my head, as it was on Farhād's.'
The candle continued, while a painful flood
each moment gushed down on his yellow cheeks:
'Pretender, this love is not your game,
as you have no patience, no strength to stand.
Untouched you shrink from a single flame,
whereas I stand still until I am consumed.
If the fire of love has scorched your wings,
look at me: it burned me from head to foot.'[32]

Auḥadī's Jām-i Jam

Of the numerous mystical maṣnavīs written since the end of the thirteenth century not one has gained the perennial fame of the works discussed so far. They cannot all, however, be dismissed as second rate or as mere imitations of the models set by the earlier great poets. Many of these later works deserve our attention because of their contributions to the continuing development of Sufi poetry. Some of these poets were quite successful for a while, before becoming overshadowed by the shining and more enduring reputations of poets like Sanā'ī, 'Aṭṭār, Rūmī and Sa'dī.

Such was the fate of Auḥadī who was born about 1270 in Marāgha (Azarbaijan) and died in 1337 at Isfahan, where he had lived for many years.[33] He was initiated in the mystical path by Auḥad ad-Dīn Kirmānī, a poet of some renown like himself. His reputation rests mainly on the long poem *Jām-i Jam* ('The Cup of Jam'), an appropriate title because, like the bowl in which the mythical king Jamshīd could behold the secrets of the world, this poems surveys the entire range of human existence. It is based on a conceptual frame which had provided an underlying structure to earlier works, but was never before applied with similar clarity. The poet describes the roads along which man during his life on earth may go either to Hell or to Paradise. In terms of the text, the circle of existence is depicted as it runs from the origin (*mabda'*) through the creative word of God, along the intinerary of earthly life (*ma'āsh*), to the final destination (*ma'ād*). The first of the poem's three parts (called *Daura*, 'cycle') is devoted to metaphysical considerations exhibiting the key rôle which mankind plays in the scheme of creation. The second, most extensive cycle deals with life in the present world. It is divided into two chapters: one treats of the ways in which the 'people of the world' spend their lives; the other, of the paths followed by the mystics who prepare themselves for the life to come. The third cycle examines the 'return' to the divine origin in terms of the final judgement awaiting every human being.

In the course of the other-worldly message he delivers, Auḥadī has also much to say about the things of this world. In the first chapter of the second *Daura*, he discusses in detail aspects of ordinary life, ranging from the service to kings, to the running of a household, sexual ethics, the education of children and the treatment of servants. The introduction of the poem contains the praise of the city of Tabriz and some of its monumental buildings, no doubt as a complimentary gesture to Auḥadī's patron, Ghiyāth ad-Dīn Muḥammad (d. 1336), the son of the famous historian Rashīd ad-Dīn, who served the Mongol rulers as a vizier. Auḥadī's main inspiration appears to have been Sanā'ī's *Ḥadīqat al-ḥaqīqa*; the *Jām-i Jam* shares with its model the metre *khafīf* and the great attention given to worldly matters in a spiritual discourse.

Khvājū Kirmānī

In the works of Abū'l-'Aṭā Kamāl ad-Dīn Maḥmūd Khvājū Kirmānī (1290–1352 or 1360) the predominant influence was Niẓāmī's *Khamsa*. Khvājū spent most of his life in Shiraz but he travelled much and, like Auḥadī, established good relations with the Mongol court at Tabriz in its final days. His best known work, the ma̱snavī *Humāy-u Humāyūn* (1331–32), was dedicated to the last Mongol ruler of Persia, Sultan Abū Sa'īd, and his vizier Ghiyāth ad-Dīn, the patron of the *Jām-i Jam*. The subject of this poem is the romance between two obscure figures from the Persian epic, developed by Khvājū into a story of love and adventure which makes use of elements borrowed from fairy tales. It is not a mystical work, unlike most of the other poems of the set of five written by Khvājū. In *Gul va Naurūz*, written in 1341–42, his intentions are made clear by the insertion of hymns on the mystics Bāyazīd Bisṭāmī (d. 874) and Abū Isḥāq Ibrāhīm Kāzarūnī (d. 1033), whom Khvājū regarded as his spiritual ancestors, and his own Master in the Kāzarūnī Sufi Order, Amīn ad-Dīn. An interesting point is that the account of Bāyazīd's visionary journey to Heaven replaces here the conventional description of the Prophet's *mi'rāj*. The poem itself tells a romantic story based on certain features of Niẓāmī's *Khusrau va*

Shīrīn. The characters are entirely fictional and carry allegorical names: a prince called Naurūz ('New Year'), the son of the king of Khurasan, falls in love with the Byzantine princess Gul ('Rose'), whose beauty is described to him by the leader of a passing caravan. During his long and arduous quest Naurūz overcomes the opposition of his father as well as numerous other obstacles. Also in this poem the influence of popular story-telling is evident. There is a didactical element as well, notably in the final part of the romance: when the couple is happily married according to the rites of 'the religion of Aḥmad' (i.e. the precursor of Islam in the primordial times in which the story is situated), they visit on their way back to Persia a convent where the sage Dānishafrūz ('the illuminator of knowledge') teaches them on the doctrine of Origin and Return, the metaphysical structure of the universe, life and death, and the fundaments of virtue.[34]

In *Rauẓat al-anvār* ('The Meadow of Lights') , written in 1342–43,[35] Khvājū closely followed Niẓāmī's *Makhzan al-asrār*. The tight structure of the latter work made it an attractive model for didactical poems. After the Indo-Persian poet Amīr Khusrau's *Maṭla' al-anvār*, completed in 1299, this was the second poem written in emulation of Niẓāmī, and there were many to follow. One year later, Khvājū produced another didactical masnavī, the *Kamāl-nāma* ('The Book of Perfection'), in the metre *khafīf*.[36] Again he emulated Niẓāmī; the poem is divided into twelve chapters, each with an identical sequence of a preliminary homily, an illustrative anecdote and a conclusion. They are preceded by the description of an allegorical journey: emerging from a 'tavern', the poet meets with Reason who summons him to an ascetic life. After his vain search for the House of God near the 'Kaaba of his heart', he sets out on a quest. He visits the natural elements Earth, Air, Water and Fire, but they all admit their impotence and refer him to higher metaphysical entities. In the end he reaches his spiritual guide who is able to provide the teaching which is transmitted to the reader in the text of the poem. This succinct specimen of a visionary tale reminds of Sanā'ī's *Sayr al-'ibād*, but also of Khaqānī's *Tuḥfat al-'Irāqayn* and 'Aṭṭār's *Muṣībat-nāma*.

Gulshan-i rāz

The short masnavī *Gulshan-i rāz* ('The Rosegarden of Mystery') by Maḥmūd Shabistarī (d. ca. 1320) was mentioned in the chapter on the *ghazal* on account of its importance to the codification of poetic idiom which became characteristic of Sufi terminology. The poem has, however, a wider significance. In the form of a catechismus, Shabistarī answers questions, giving first a theoretical exposition and then illustrations to the point discussed by means of similes and parables. The general topic is the doctrine of man's perfection through gnosis. A number of cosmological, psychological and metaphysical issues are dealt with, but also matters particular to the Sufi tradition, for example, the problems posed by expressions of identification with the Divine Being. In this work, as well as in another masnavī on Sufi theology, the *Sa'ādat-nāma*, the influence of Ibn al-'Arabī's doctrine of the Unity of Being is evident. Shabistarī's little poem was not only successful in the area of Persian culture but also in the West.[37]

According to a not quite reliable tradition, the man who put the questions answered in *Gulshan-i rāz* would have been another writer of mystical poetry, Ḥusaynī Sādāt Amīr (d. after 1328).[38] Although he was held in high esteem by his contemporaries, and even by following generations, his works, among which the masnavīs *Zād al-musāfirīn* ('Provisions for Travellers') and *Kanz ar-rumūz* ('The Treasury of Symbols') are the most important, are little known now.

Sufi practices

Most works in the tradition of masnavī writing deal with mystical ideas and spiritual education, far less with Sufi practices. There are, however, exceptions. One of these is *Kārnāma-yi auqāf*, a poem of less than 400 distichs which was composed at the occasion of the New Year festival of 667 AH (1269) by Pūr-i Bahā, a court poet of the Mongol rulers. It is a satirical work, criticising the misuse of the institution of the pious foundation on which Sufis often had to rely for their subsistence. The little poem is especially interesting because of a description of a Ḥaydarī dervish, who belonged to one of the antinomian groups; they are often alluded to in a figurative way, but hardly ever depicted from reality.[39]

In 1347–48 Khaṭīb-i Fārisī of Shiraz wrote a hagiography in masnavī on the Persian Sufi Jamāl ad-Dīn Sāvī (d. ca. 1232). After his conversion to radical ascetism, Jamāl ad-Dīn became the master of a group of dervishes in Damascus, whom the author identifies as 'qalandars'. They radically rejected both the ties to the present world and pious concerns with salvation in the afterlife. The visible tokens of their practices were the shaving of hair, beard, moustache and eyebrows, and their nakedness except for a loin cloth or a coarse woollen garment called a 'sack' (*jaulaq*). A repeated phrase in the poem summarises the meaning of their behaviour:

Come, let us wash our hands from this world,
And say four takbīrs[40] *as qalandars are wont to.*

They actually lived the life of the qalandar which Persian poets since the early twelfth century had depicted in literature.[41]

The practices of a Sufi community are also reflected in de masnavīs of 'Imād ad-Dīn 'Alī (d. 1371), also known as Faqīh-i Kirmānī, 'the jurisprudent of Kirman', discussed already as a poet of *ghazals*. Like many mystics of his times, he did not neglect the relations with the powers of the world. He dedicated works to Shāh Shujā', a ruler of Shiraz who was also a patron of Ḥāfiẓ, and to the Mongol vizier Ghiyāth ad-Dīn, a great supporter of mystical poets as we saw already.

The five masnavīs of 'Imād-i Faqīh are sometimes named *Panj Ganj* ('Five Treasures') collectively. They are remarkable both for their forms and their contents. The *Ṣuḥbat-nāma* ('The Book of Company'), written in 1330, is modelled on Sa'dī's *Būstān* as far as the choice of the metre and the division of the poem into ten brief chapters is concerned. Like Sa'dī, he first turns his attention to the ruling class, emphasising the virtues of generosity and justice proper to their status. The subject-matter of the other chapters is different, however: 'Imād treats of the rules of behaviour (*ādāb*) for groups of people who are distinguished by their attitudes towards the spiritual life. After Sufis, scholars and the 'people of the world', he talks about those who run a convent, those who have adopted a wandering life and those who follow the code of chivalry, known as *futuvvat*, in the daily life of a Sufi community.[42] The last three chapters are concerned with mystical love and the way it is represented in the poems sung by the singers of the convent. The introduction to this 'educational book' (*tarbiyat-nāma*), as the poet characterises it, contains autobiographical information.[43]

The *Ṣafā-nāma* ('The Book of Purity'), also entitled *Mu'nis al-abrār* ('The Companion of the Pious'), completed in 1364, and imitating outwardly Niẓāmī's *Makhzan al-asrār*, is a work of 'Imād's old age. Prominent themes are complaints about the tyranny of Time, and the account of a visionary experience in the last of the three chapters. The poet dreams first about the Prophet and 'Alī, and then meets with Khiẕr. He relates how he experiences the throes of death and the bodily ressurrection prior to his encounter with a deceased Sufi sheikh, whose life was described in a preceding chapter of the poem.[44] The other poems of this set are merely of literary interest and are characteristic of 'Imād's concern for good relations with the courts.

A practical aim may also be attributed to two brief masnavīs by the mystic Qāsim-i Anvār (1356–1433). Although they deal with theoretical questions, their concise form and unadorned language mark them as tools for basic instruction to adepts. In *Ṣad maqām dar iṣṭilāḥ-i ṣūfīya* ('A Hundred Stages in Sufi Terminology') the mystical path, from 'the awakening to the realisation of Oneness' is mapped out by a vocabulary of terms proper to it. Such catalogues were made often in this period, no doubt for the purpose of memorisation. The other work by Qāsim, *Anīs al-'ārifīn* ('The Companion of the Mystics'), in about 600 distichs, is a catechismus of Sufi psychology providing answers on questions concerning the lower soul (*nafs*), the spirit (*rūḥ*), the heart, reason and mystical love. The poet elaborates in particular on the sin of 'showing off piety' (*riyā*). Whosoever falls a victim to this temptation, is compared to someone who supposes the devil's urinating on his head to be a (blessing) rainfall. Instead, the adept is urged to save his heart from the 'hand of the demon' by making it into a receptacle for the outpourings of the spirit. The state of purification is exemplified by the mystic Ṣafī ad-Dīn of Ardabil, the ancestor of the later Safavid Shahs, who brought the poet Sa'dī to the confession that 'his bird could not make his nest' at such a high level. One is reminded of the latter's *Būstān*, when Qāsim-i Anvār in concluding his poem resorts to the parable of the moth and the candle to demonstrate the overpowering force of love.

Mystical allegories

A standardisation of mystical language, together with an increasingly overt use of allegory, these had become distinctive features of the Sufi masnavī in the course of the fourteenth century. They are even more noticeable in the next century, which was the period of the Timurids in the political history of Persia. No poet could better illustrate these tendencies than Muḥammad Yaḥyā ibn Sībak, better known as Fattāḥī (d. ab. 1448), who spent a secluded life in his native Nishapur. The *Dastūr al-'ushshāq* ('The Councillor of the Lovers'), a masnavī of 5,000 distichs which was completed in 1436, contains a romance full of adventures not unlike Khvājū's *Gul va Naurūz*. However, in this case the allegorisation of the story has been carried out to its final consequences. Not only the personal names but also the geographical names are all derived from the vocabulary of love poetry and the psychology related to it. The mention of only the most important protagonists should suffice to characterise the story: a prince Heart (*Dil*), the son of King Reason (*'Aql*) who reigns in the West in a castle called Body (*Badan*), sets out to win the hand of Beauty (*Ḥusn*), the daughter of King Love (*'Ishq*), who is the ruler of the East. The princess lives in the city Complexion (*Dīdār*), which has a garden called Cheeks (*Rukhsār*) and a fountain by the name of Mouth (*Famm*). In order to clarify this intricate allegory Fattāḥī also wrote a condensed version in prose under the title *Ḥusn va Dil*.

The predominance of the allegory as it is exemplified in the work of Fattāḥī and many of his contemporaries led inevitably to a rigidity which reduced the expressive force of Sufi poetry. Earlier poets used their stories and lyrical motives much more freely as they were not bound to pre-defined notions attached to them in a catalogue fashion. It is not accidental that in this last stage of medieval literature small vocabularies of Sufi terminology were composed by which one could decode poetical images to a lexical meaning.

To some extent a compensation for this loss of vitality was sought in a greater concern for rhetorical finesse. This was also the period when poets exerted themselves to apply intricate verbal tricks to their works. The poem *Siḥr-i ḥalāl* ('Lawful Magic') by Ahlī of Shiraz (d.1535) was written in double rhyming verses and can be scanned according to two different metres.

Although some of the allegorical ma̱snavīs did enjoy a certain popularity for some time, nearly all of them fell into oblivion eventually. One of the earliest was *Mihr va Mushtarī*, written by Shams ad-Dīn Muḥammad 'Aṣṣār (d. 1377), in which the Sun and the Planet Jupiter play the leading parts. More abstract is the pair of lovers Regarder (*Nāẓir*) and Regarded (*Manẓūr*) in *Majma' al-baḥrayn* ('The Confluence of the Two Seas') by Kātibī of Turshiz (d. 1434–35). Well-known lyrical motives were personified in *Gūy va Chaugān* ('The Ball and the Polo Stick') by 'Ārifī (d. 1449) which betrays its real meaning in the alternative title *Ḥāl-nāma* ('Book of Ecstasy'), and *Sham' va Parvāna* ('The Candle and the Moth') by the aforementioned poet Ahlī. In *Shāh va Gadā*, Hilālī (d. 1529) used the contrast between 'King and Beggar' as an allegory of the relationship between God and the mystical lover.

The Seven Thrones of Jāmī

The contributions of Jāmī (1414–92) to Sufi ma̱snavī poetry are not devoid of original features. In his *Haft Aurang* ('The Seven Thrones', which in Persian also denotes the constellation of the Great Bear), he extended Niẓāmī's pattern of five poems to a set of seven. Only two of his poems, *Laylā va Majnūn* and *Khirad-nāma-yi Iskandarī* ('The Book of Alexander's Wisdom'), have subjects represented in the *Khamsa* of his predecessor. The story of Khusrau and Shīrīn is replaced by the love between Yūsuf and Zulaykhā, as the wife of the Egyptian minister Pothifar is known in the Islamic tradition. This subject was hallowed by its occurrence in the Koran (Sūra xii) and is frequently alluded to in lyrical poetry. The only earlier medieval treatment in a ma̱snavī which has survived merely relates the pious legends about the Prophet Joseph and cannot be regarded as a mystical work.[45] In the hands of Jāmī it became a magnificent tale of mystical love. Although the allegorical meaning is never left out of sight, the narrative is not entirely dominated by this and has a value of its own.[46]

The same assertion could not be made with regard to *Salāmān va Absāl,* simply because in this case the story, of Hellenistic origin, was already used by Ibn Sīnā (Avicenna) as a philosophical parable in Arabic prose. Salāmān, born as the son of the King of Greece but not from a mother, falls in love with his nurse Absāl who is twenty years older than he. The lovers flee to a paradisical island. There they throw themselves into a fire from which only Salāmān escapes, unwounded and purged of his attachements to this world.

In an epilogue, Jāmī provides the key to the allegory. The king of Greece is unmasked as the Active Intelligence, the mediator between the higher intelligences and the human intellect. The stream of ideas transmitted by him is represented by the wise councillor of the King. The miraculous birth of Salāmān refers to the non-material origin of the human soul. The coexistence between the rational soul and the body, which should end in their total separation after the development of the soul has been completed constitutes the story of the poem. Absāl, who had to be destroyed in the process, is the body which is dominated by its lusts.

The set of seven poems is completed by three poems which are truly didactical. In *Silsilat az̲-z̲ahab* ('The Golden Chain'), written in the metre *khafīf*, the remote example is Sanā'ī's *Ḥadīqat al-ḥaqīqa*, but Jāmī's poem is far from being a close imitation. The first of its three parts treats of the essentials of Sufi education, including an *I'tiqād-nāma* ('Book of Credo') summarising the main tenets of orthodox Islam and written at the request of the sheikh of the Naqshbandī Order 'Ubayd-Allāh Aḥrār. The second part of the poem is devoted to mystical love and contains many exemplary tales; the last part is a mirror-for-princes written at the request of the Ottoman Sultan Bāyezid II (reigned 1481–1512).[47] *Tuḥfat al-aḥrār* ('The Gift for the Noble') and *Subḥat al-asrār* ('The Rosary of the Secrets') are both designed on the model of Nizāmī's *Makhzan al-asrār* and deal with a wide range of subjects relevant to the way of life of the mystics, but also pay attention to the proper behaviour of kings, scholars and poets.

With the seven poems of Jāmī we have reached to boundary which we set for our discussion. At the beginning of the sixteenth century, dramatic changes took place in the political and cultural life of Persia. They brought in many respects a new orientation and a shift of emphasis also in spiritual life. Since Imami Shi'ism became the religion of the rulers and of the people, the role of Sufism became less dominating than it had been during the Middle Ages. However, it did not disappear altogether, nor did the literature which for centuries had expressed Sufism in such a splendid manner. Yet, it cannot be denied that the great Sufi poets and their works were never surpassed in subsequent centuries.

Notes

1. See G. Lazard, *Les premiers poètes persans*, Paris-Tehran 1963, I, pp. 27–30 and 100–26. On Persian mas̲navīs in general see: EI s.v. Mat̲h̲nawī.1.

2. The *Raushanā'ī-nāma* was first edited and translated (into German) in 1879–80 by H. Ethé; see further De Blois, PL, v/1, pp. 206–11.
3. On the Active Intelligence, called *al-'aql al-fa''āl* in Islamic philosophy, see EI, s.v. 'Aḳl.
4. Koran, Sūra vii, 54 and Sūra x, 3, referring to God's taking control of His creation after He had brought it into being in six days.
5. *Sayr al-'ibād ilā'l-ma'ād*, Ms. Bağdatli Vehbi No. 1672, ff. 182b–183a.
6. This copy of the poem, now kept in the Süleymaniye Library, Istanbul, under the bookmark Bağdatli Vehbi No. 1672, was made to the order of a goldsmith in Konya. A much expanded form of the poem was published by M. Raẓavī; see also De Bruijn, *Of Piety and Poetry*, pp. 119–39.
7. On Khāqānī's masnavī see the studies by Beelaert, mentioned above in Chapter 2, n. 17.
8. The poem is described by Bo Utas, 'A journey to the other world according to the Lantern of Spirits', in *Bulletin of the Asia Institute*, New series, Vol. 4 (1990), pp. 307–11; for an analysis of its manuscript tradition see: the same, in *Barg-i sabz / A Green Leaf, Acta Iranica* 28, *Hommages and Opera Minora* 12, Leiden 1988, pp. 237–52.
9. On Baqlī's mysticism see: Carl W. Ernst, *Words of Ecstasy in Sufism*, Albany 1985.
10. *Kitāb 'abhar al-'āshiqīn*, pp. 6–8; cf. *Ḥadīqa*, ed. M. Raẓavī, pp. 346 ff.
11. B. Utas based on this poem a statistical study of Sufi terminology, *A Persian Sufi poem: Vocabulary and terminology*, London-Malmö 1978.
12. Sections from Niẓāmī's introduction to this poem were translated into German by J.Chr. Bürgel, 'Niẓāmī über Sprache und Dichtung', in *Islamwissenschaftliche Abhandlungen, Fritz Meier zum 60sten Geburtstag gewidmet*, Wiesbaden 1974, pp. 9–28. On the discussion about religion and poetry see also: J.T.P. de Bruijn, 'Comparative notes on Sanā'ī and 'Attār' in L. Lewisohn (ed.), *Classical Persian Sufism*, pp. 361–79.
13. EI, s.v. Madjnūn Laylā. 2.
14. For a recent survey of editions and translations of Niẓāmī's masnavī's see De Blois, PL, v/2, pp. 438–95.
15. S. Nafīsī, *Justujū dar aḥvāl va āsār-i Farīd ad-Dīn 'Aṭṭār*, Tehran 1320/1941; see also H. Ritter, EI, s.v. 'Aṭṭār and the survey of his works by De Blois, PL, v/2, pp. 270–318.
16. At early as the late fourteenth century the *Ushtur-nāma* was accepted as a genuine work by 'Aṭṭār. The oldest manuscript, dated 786 A.H/1384, is kept in the Leiden University Library, No. 310/2.
17. According to H. Ritter, the *Haylāj-nāma* is 'a poor imitation of the second part of the *Ushtur-nāma*'.

18. *Le langage des oiseaux*, Paris 1857.
19. See Hanns-Peter Schmidt, 'The sēnmurw. Of birds and dogs and bats' in *Persica*, ix, 1980, pp. 1–85; CHI, Vol. 3(1), p. 346.
20. He is mentioned also in lyrical poems as an example of the antinomian attitude; see the ghazal by Ḥāfiẓ analysed in Chapter 4.
21. *Le Livre des Secrets*, Paris 1985, pp. 9–11.
22. 'The religious mathnavīs of Farīd al-Dīn 'Aṭṭār' in *IRAN* 17 (1979), pp. 9f.
23. Ed. T. Yazici, pp. 739–44.
24. *The Mathnawí*, vii, pp. 8–9.
25. 'Mesnevī'nin onsekiz beytinin mânâsi' [The meaning of the eighteen distichs of the Masnavī], in *Fuad Köprülü Armağani*, Istanbul 1953, pp. 37–50 (in Turkish).
26. *The Mathnawí*, i, lines 2–8.
27. See also William C. Chittick, *The Sufi Path of Love. The Spiritual Teachings of Rumi*, Albany 1983.
28. *The Mathnawí*, i, lines 139–43.
29. Cf. above, Chapter 3, p. 58.
30. Abū'l-Fayḍ Thaubān ibn Ibrāhīm Dhū'n-Nūn (d. 861), one of great early Sufis who lived in Egypt, equated in some of his statements mystical knowledge (*ma'rifa*) with the ecstatic experience of love; see: Schimmel, *Mystical Dimensions*, pp. 42–47.
31. *Valad-nāma*, p. 53.
32. *Būstān*, p. 114.
33. Browne, LHP, iii, pp. 141–46; Arberry, CPL, pp. 305–08; Rypka, HIL, p. 254.
34. Khvājū Kirmānī, *Khamsa*, pp. 469–722.
35. Op.cit., pp. 1–98.
36. Op. cit., pp. 101–98.
37. It was used as a source by one of the earliest students of Islamic mysticism in the West, F.A.D. Tholuck (*Ssufismus*, Berlin 1821).
38. K.A. Nizami, EI, s.v. Ḥusaynī Sādāt Amīr.
39. The poem has been published in transcription together with a German translation by Birgitt Hoffmann, in *Proceedings of the First European Conference of Iranian Studies*, Rome 1990, pp. 409–85.
40. I.e.: 'say four times *Allāhu akbar*', as it is the custom at a funeral.
41. See above the section on 'unbelievers and qalandars', Chapter 3, pp. 71–76.
42. This section was edited and transated into German by Herbert W. Duda in *Archiv Orientální*, vi, 1934, pp. 112–24.
43. 'Imād ad-Dīn, *Panj ganj*, pp. 94–148.
44. Op.cit., pp. 19–91.

45. Partly edited by H. Ethé, Oxford 1908, as a work of Firdausī, an attribution now no longer accepted; cf. De Blois, PL, v/2, pp. 576 ff.
46. For a translated passage from the introduction of this poem see Chapter 1, *in fine*.
47. *Haft Aurang*, pp. 2–183.

Select Bibliography

A.J. Arberry, *Sufism. An Account of the Mystics of Islam*, London 1950

Idem, *The Koran Interpreted*, 2 vols., London-New York 1954–56.

Idem, *Classical Persian Literature*, London 1958 [CPL].

Julian Baldick, 'Persian Sūfī Poetry up to the Fifteenth Century', in George Morrison (ed.), *History of Persian Literature*, Leiden-Köln 1981, pp. 111–32.

Amin Banani, Richard Hovannisian and Georges Sabagh (ed.), *Poetry and Mysticism in Islam. The Heritage of Rūmī*, Cambridge 1994.

Edward G. Browne, *A Literary History of Persia*, 4 vols., London-Cambridge 1902–25 [LHP].

J.T.P. de Bruijn, *Of Pietry and Poetry: The Interaction of Religion and Literature in the Life and Works of Ḥakīm Sanā'ī of Ghazna*, Leiden 1983.

Johann Christoph Bürgel, *The Feather of Simurgh: The 'Licit Magic' of the Arts in Medieval Islam*, New York-London 1988.

The Cambridge History of Iran, 7 vols., Cambridge 1968–91 [CHI].

The Encyclopaedia of Islam. New Edition, Leiden 1960- [EI].

Encyclopaedia Iranica, ed by Ehsan Yarshater, London-Costa Mesa 1982- [Enc.Ir.].

Leonard Lewisohn (ed.), *The Legacy of Mediaeval Persian Sufism*, London-New York 1992.

Idem (ed.), *Classical Persian Sufism: from its Origins to Rumi*, London-New York 1993.

Reynold A. Nicholson, *The Mystics of Islam*, London 1914.

Idem, *Studies in Islamic Mysticism*, Cambridge 1921; reprint 1967.

Hellmut Ritter, *Das Meer der Seele. Mensch, Welt und Gott in den Geschichten des Farīduddīn 'Aṭṭār*, Leiden 1955; reprint 1980.

Jan Rypka, et al., *History of Iranian Literature*, Dordrecht 1968 [HIL].

Annemarie Schimmel, *Mystical Dimensions of Islam*, Chapel Hill 1975.

Eadem, *The Triumphal Sun. A Study of the Works of Jalāloddin Rumi*, London-The Hague 1978.

Eadem, *As Through a Veil: Mystical Poetry in Islam*, New York 1982.

Eadem, *And Muhammad is His Messenger*, Chapel Hill and London 1985.

C.A. Storey, *Persian Literature. A Bio-bibliographical Survey*, London 1927- ; continued by François de Blois, Volume v/1 and 2, London 1992–94 [PL].

Ehsan Yarshater (ed.), *Persian Literature*, Albany 1988.

Persian texts: editions and English translations

Abū Sa'īd ibn Abī'l-Khayr:

'Die Rubâ'îs des Abû Sa'îd bin Abulchair', in *Sitzungsberichte der philosophisch-philologischen und historischen Classe der köninglichen bayerischen Akademie der Wissenschaften*, München 1875, ii, pp. 145–68, and 1878, ii, pp. 38–70 (see also Browne, LHP, ii, pp. 261–64); *Sukhanān-i manẓūm-i Abū Sa'īd-i Abū'l-Khayr*, ed. by S. Nafīsī, Tehran 1334 (1955).

Afẕal ad-Dīn, Bābā:

Rubā'īyāt. Les quatrains . . . précédé d'une étude sur la vie et l'oeuvre du poète, ed. by S. Nafīsī, Tehran 1311 (1933); M. Mīnuvī and Mahdawī, *Muṣannafāt-i Afẕal ad-Dīn Muḥammad-i Maraqī Kāshānī*, 2 vols. Tehran 1331–7 (1952–8).

Aflākī, Sham ad-Dīn Aḥmad:

Manāqib al-'ārifīn, ed. by Tahsin Yazici, 2 vols., 2nd ed., Ankara 1980.

'Ārifī:

Gūy-u chaugān yā Ḥāl-nāma, ed. and translated by R.S. Greenshields, London 1931–32.

'Aṭṭār, Farīd ad-Dīn:

Asrār-nāma, ed. by Ṣādiq Gauharīn, Tehran 1338 (1959).

Bīsar-nāma, ed. by A. Khushnavīs 'Imād, Tehran 1362 (1983); published together with other texts of uncertain authorship.

Dīvān-i ghazalīyāt va qaṣāyid-i 'Aṭṭār, ed. Taqī Tafaẕẕulī, Tehran 1341 (1962).

Haylāj-nāma, ed. by A. Khushnavīs 'Imād, 2nd ed., Tehran 1371 (1992).

Ilāhī-nāma, ed. by Hellmut Ritter, Leipzig 1940; ed. by F. Rūḥānī, Tehran 1351 (1972); translated by J.A. Boyle, *The Ilāhī-nāma or Book of God*, Manchester 1976.

Majmū'a-yi rubā'īyāt [Mukhtār-nāma], ed. by M.R. Shafī'ī Kadkanī, Tehran 1358 (1979).
Manṭiq aṭ-ṭayr, ed. by Ṣādiq Gauharīn, 2nd ed., Tehran 1348 (1969); translated by Afkham Darbandi and Dick Davis, *The Conference of the Birds*, Penguin Classics, 1984.
Muṣībat-nāma, ed. by Nūrānī Viṣāl, Tehran 1338 (1959).
Tazkirat al-auliyā', ed. by Reynold A. Nicholson, Leiden-London 1905–07; selections translated by A.J. Arberry, *Muslim Saints and Mystics*, London 1966.
Ushtur-nāma, ed. by Mehdī Muḥaqqiq, Part 1, Tehran 1339 (1960).

Auḥadī Marāghī:
Jām-i Jam, ed. by Sa'īd Nafīsī, in *Kullīyāt-i Auḥadī-yi Isfahānī ma'rūf ba-Marāghī*, Tehran 1340/1961, pp. 482–673.

Ghazālī, Aḥmad:
Kitāb-i Savāniḥ (Aphorismen über die Liebe), ed. by H.Ritter, Leipzig-Istanbul 1942; translated by Nasrollah Pourjavady, London 1968.

Ghazālī, Muḥammad:
Kīmiyā-yi sa'ādat, ed. A. Arām, Tehran 1352 (1973).

Ḥasan-i Ghaznavī Ashraf, Sayyid:
Dīvān, ed. by Mudarris Razavī, 2nd ed., Tehran 1363 (1984).

Ḥāfiẓ:
Dīvān, ed. by Parvīz Nātil Khānlarī, 2nd ed., Tehran 1362 (1984); A.J. Arberry, *Fifty Poems of Ḥāfiẓ*, Cambridge 1953 (texts and translations).

Hujvīrī, 'Alī ibn 'Usmān al-Jullābī:
The Kashf al-maḥjúb. The oldest Persian treatise on Sufism, translated by Reynold A. Nicholson, London 1911; several times reprinted.

Ibn-i Yamīn:
E.H. Roswell, *Ibn Yamin, Persice Ibn-i Yamin, 100 short poems. The Persian text with paraphrases*, London 1933.

'Imād ad-Dīn Faqīh-i Kirmānī:
Dīvān, ed. by Rukn ad-Dīn Humāyūn-Farrukh, Tehran 1348 (1969).
Panj ganj, ed by Rukn ad-Dīn Humāyūn-Farrukh, Tehran 2537 (1978).

'Irāqī:
Kullīyāt, ed. by Sa'īd Nafīsī, Tehran 1338 (1959).

Jāmī, Mullā 'Abd ar-Raḥmān:
Masnavī-yi Haft Aurang, ed. by Mudarris Gīlānī, Tehran 1337 (1958).

Kamāl ad-Dīn Ismā'īl Iṣfahānī:
Dīvān-i Khallāq al-ma'ānī, ed by Ḥusayn Baḥr al-'ulūmī, Tehran 1348 (1969).
Kāshānī, 'Izz ad-Dīn Maḥmūd:
Kunūz al-asrār va rumūz al-aḥrār ('Ishq-nāma), ed. by A. Mujāhid, *Shurūḥ-i Savāniḥ*, Tehran 1372 (1994), pp. 3–30.
Kay-Kā'ūs:
Qābūs-nāma, ed. by Ghulām-Ḥusayn Yūsufī, Tehran 1345 (1967).
Khāqānī:
Dīvān-i Khāqānī-yi Sharvānī, ed. Ẓiyā ad-Dīn Sajjādī, Tehran 1338 (1959).
Tuḥfat al-'Irāqayn, ed. by Yaḥyā Qarīb, Tehran 1333 (1955).
Khatīb-i Fārisī:
Manāqib-i Jamāl ad-Dīn Sāvī, ed. by Tahsin Yazici, Ankara 1972; ed. by Ḥusayn Zarrīnkūb, Tehran 1985.
Khusrau Dihlavī, Amīr:
Maṭla' al-anvār, ed. by T.A. Magerramova, Moscow 1975.
Khvājū Kirmānī:
Dīvān, ed. by A. Suhaylī-Khvānsārī, Tehran 1336 (1957).
Khamsa-yi Khvājū Kirmānī, ed. Sa'īd Niyāz-i Kirmānī, Kirman 1370 (1991).
Maghribī, Muḥammad Shīrīn:
Dīvān, ed. by Leonard Lewisohn, Tehran-London 1993.
Muḥammad ibn Munavvar:
Asrār at-tauḥīd fī maqāmāt ash-Shaykh Abī Sa'īd, ed. M.R. Shafī'ī-Kadkanī, Tehran 1366 (1987); translated by John O'Kane, *The Secrets of God's Mystical Oneness*, Costa Mesa 1992.
Najm ad-Dīn Dāya:
Mirṣād al-'ibād min al-mabda' ilā'l-ma'ād, ed. M.A.Riyāḥī, Tehran 1352 (1973); *The Path of God's Bondsmen from Origin to Return: Mersad al-'Ebad*, translated by H.Algar, Delmar NY 1980.
Nakhjavānī, Aḥmad ibn al-Ḥasan ibn Muḥammad:
Ṭarīq at-taḥqīq, ed. by Bo Utas, Lund 1973.
Nāṣir-i Khusrau:
Dīvān-i ash'ār, ed. by Naṣr-Allāh Taqavī, Tehran 13047/1925–8, repeatedly reprinted; *Forty poems from the Divan*, translated by Peter Lamborn Wilson and Gholam Reza Aavani, Tehran 1977.
Raushanā'ī-nāma, edited (and translated into German) by Hermann Ethé, in *Zeitschrift der Deutschen Morgenländischen Gesellschaft* 33, 1879, pp. 645–64, and 34, 1880, pp. 428–64, 617–42; reprinted Berlin 1922, together with the *Safar-nāma*; *Dīvān*, pp. 511–42.

Niẓāmī:

Khamsa, ed. by Vaḥīd Dastgirdī, Tehran 1313–8 (1934–9) and reprints.

Makhzan al-asrār, ed. by A.A. Alizade, Baku 1960; ed. by Bihrūz Sarvatīyān, Tehran 1363 (1984); translated by G.H. Darab, *The Treasury of Mysteries*, London 1945.

Qāsim-i Anvār:

Kullīyāt, ed. by Sa'īd Nafīsī, Tehran 1337 (1958).

Qivāmī-yi Rāzī:

Divān, ed. by Mīr Jalāl ad-Dīn Muḥaddiṣ, Tehran 1374/1334 (1955)

Rūmī, Jalāl ad-Dīn:

Kullīyāt-i Shams yā Dīvān-i kabīr, ed. by Badī' az-zamān Furūzānfar, 10 vols., Tehran 1336 (1957) ff.; Reynold A. Nicholson, *Selected poems from the Dīvāni Shamsi Tabrīz*, Cambridge 1898 (with translations); A.J. Arberry, *The Rubā'iyāt of Jalāl al-Dīn Rūmī*, London 1949.

The Mathnawí of Jalálu'ddín Rúmí, ed. by Reynold A. Nicholson, 8 vols., Leiden-London 1925–40 (Persian text, English translation and commentary); selections translated by R.A. Nicholson, *Tales of Mystic Meaning*, London 1931, by A.J. Arberry in *Tales from the Masnavi*, London 1962 and *More tales from the Masnavi*, London 1963.

Rūzbihān-i Baqlī:

Kitāb 'abhar al-'āshiqīn, ed. by H. Corbin and M. Mu'īn, Tehran-Paris 1958.

Sa'dī:

Kullīyāt, ed. by Muḥammad 'Alī Furūghī, Tehran 1337 (1958), collected works, including the *ghazals*; *Ṭayyibāt*, ed. and translated by L.W. King, Calcutta 1919–21 and London 1926; translations by the same from the *Badāyi'*, Berlin 1304/1925.

Būstān, ed. by Ghulām-Ḥusayn Yūsufī, 2nd ed., Tehran 1363 (1984); translated by G.M. Wickens, *Morals Pointed and Tales Adorned*, Leiden 1974.

Salmān-i Sāvajī:

Dīvān, ed. by Manṣūr Mushfiq, Tehran 1336 (1957).

Sanā'ī:

Dīvān, ed. by Mudarris Raẓavī, 2nd ed., Tehran 1341/1962; *Tāziyānahā-yi sulūk* ['Whips for travelling the Path'], annotated anthology from the *zuhdīyāt* by M. R. Shafī'ī Kadkanī,Tehran 1371/1993.

Ḥadīqat al-ḥaqīqa va sharī'at aṭ-ṭarīqa, ed. by Mudarris Raẓavī, Tehran 1313 (1950); *Kullīyāt-i ash'ār-i ḥakīm Sanā'ī-yi Ghaznavī*, ed. by 'Alī Asghar Bashīr, Kabul 1356 (1977), pp. 2–280 (facsimile-edition of an ancient ms. in Kabul); *Fakhrī-nāma*, Ms. Bağdatli Vehbi (Istanbul) No. 1672, ff. 1b–179a.

Sayr al-'ibād ilā'l-ma'ād, Ms. Bağdatli Vehbi No. 1672, ff. 179b–203b. A not quite satisfactory edition of the text and an ancient commentary can be found in *Masnavīhā-yi Ḥakīm Sanā'ī*, ed. by M. Raẕavī, Tehran 1348/1969, pp. 181–316; this collection also contains a number of masnavīs that were mistakenly attributed to Sanā'ī (cf. Utas, *Ṭarīq ut-taḥqīq*, *passim*, and De Bruijn, *Of Piety and Poetry*, pp. 113–18).

Shabistarī, Maḥmūd:

Gulshan-i Rāz, The Mystic Rose Garden, ed. and translated by E.H. Whinfield, London 1880, reprinted Lahore 1978.

Sulṭān Valad:

Valad-nāma, ed. J. Humā'ī, Tehran 1316 (1937).

Ṭāhir, Bābā:

The first modern collection was published by Clément Huart in *Journal asiatique* (1889, 1908); translated by Edward Heron-Allen and Elizabeth Curtis Brenton, *The Lament of Bābā-Tāhir*, London 1902, and by A.J. Arberry, *Poems of a Persian Ṣūfī*, Cambridge 1937.

Index

'Abhar al 'āshiqın 70, 95
Abraham 105
Abū Bakr (Caliph) 32, 93
Abū Bakr ibn Sa'd-i Zangī (ruler of Shiraz) 113
Abū Ḥanīfa 36, 42, 93
Abū Isḥāq Ibrāhīm Kāzarūnī 116
Abū'l-'Atāhiya 30
Abū Nuwās 30
Abū Sa'īd ibn Abī'l-Khayr **16–19**, 24, 74, 75
Abū Sa'īd (Mongol ruler) 116
Abū Shakūr 85, 114
Adam 24, 105
Āfarīn-nāma 85
Aflākī, Shams ad-Dīn Aḥmad 108, 109
Ahlī 122
Ahl-i Ḥaqq 13
Aḥmad see Muḥammad
Aḥrār, 'Ubayd-Allāh 25, 124
Algar, H. 27
'Alī ibn Abī Ṭālib 32, 33, 48, 60, 93, 120
Ali-Shah, O. 27
amānat 107
Amīn ad-Dīn (sheikh of the Kāzarūnīya) 116
andarz-nāmag 86
Anīs al-'ārifīn **120–121**
Anṣārī, 'Abd Allāh 37, 74
Anvarī 44, 57
'aql al-fa''āl, al- 125
Arabian Nights 100
Arberry, A.J. 1, 26, 27, 47, 49, 50, 54, 77, 81, 82, 83
'Ārifī 122
Ascension to Heaven see *mi'rāj*
'āshiq 65
Asrāfīl 105
Asrār at-tauḥīd fī maqāmāt ash-shaykh Abī Sa'īd 16, 18, 24
Asrār-nāma **106–108**
'Aṣṣār, Shams ad-Dīn Muḥammad 122
Ateş, A. 109
'Aṭṭār, Farīd ad-Dīn 12, **21–23**, **47–48**, **57**, 58, 71, 74, 80, 98, **99–108**, 109, 115, 117
'Aufī 33
Auḥad ad-Dīn Kirmānī 21, 95, 115

Auḥadī **115–116**
Avicenna see Ibn-i Sīnā
'Awārif al-ma 'ārif 73
'Ayn al-Quẕāt Hamadānī 24, 41, 70
'Azrā'īl 105

Bābā Afẕal (Afẕal ad-Dīn Kāshī/ Maraqī) **19–20**
Bābā Fighānī 62
Bābā Ṭāhir 'Uryān **13–16**, 74
Badā'i' 59
Bahā ad-Dīn Valad 57, 108
Bahā ad-Dīn Zakarīyā 59
Bahrāmshāh (Ghaznavid Sultan) 37, 38, 56, 57, 92
Bahrāmshāh (ruler of Erzincan) 97
Bāqiya-yi nāqiya 60
Bardāsīrī, Shams ad-Dīn Muḥammad Īl-Ṭughān 95
Bausani, A. 81
Bāyazīd Bistamī 116
Bāyezīd II (Ottoman Sultan) 124
Beelaert, A.L.F.A. 49, 125
Bilqīs 102
Bīsar-nāma 100
Bishr-i Yāsīn 17
Blois, F de 27, 49, 125, 126
Bodleian Library 10
Bowen, J.C.E. 27
Boyle, A.J. 27, 106
Brethren of Purity 89
Browne, E.G. 27, 49, 50, 82
Bruijn, J.T.P. de 50, 82, 83, 125
Bū Ṣāliḥ (reciter) 24
Bürgel, J. Chr. 82, 125
Burhān ad-Dīn Muḥaqqiq 112
Būstān 59, **113–114**, 121

Chistī Order 59, 60
Chittick, W. 126
Classical Persian Literature 2

Dashtī, 'Alī 27
Dastgirdī, Vaḥīd 14
Dastūr al-'ushshāq 121
David 105
Denison Ross, E. 27
Dhū'n-Nūn 4, 113, 126
Dīvān-i kabīr 58
du-baytī 7, 14
Duda, H.W. 126
duvāzdah-band 49

Elwell-Sutton, L.P. 26, 27
Ernst, C.W. 125
Ethé, H. 18, 125, 126

Fakhr ad-Dīn Rāzī 10
Fakhrī-nāma 10
Farhād 114
Farīd ad-Dīn 'Aṭṭār see 'Aṭṭar
Fātiḥat ash-shabāb 62
Fāṭima (wife of Sulṭān Valad) 112
Fattāḥī, Muḥammad Yaḥyā ibn Sībak **121–122**
Fīhi mā fīhi 112
Firdausī 83, 85, 114
FitzGerald, Edward 9, 10, 11, 27
Fouchécour, C.-H. de 26

Gabriel 105
ghazal **51–83** and *passim*
Ghazālī, Aḥmad 23, 52, 59, 69, 70, **74–75**, 101
Ghazālī, Muḥammad 69, 82, 101
Ghazalīyāt-i qadīm 59
Ghiyāth ad-Dīn Muḥammad 116, 119

Ghurrat al-kamāl 60
Glünz, M. 49, 82
Graves, Robert 11
Gul va Naurūz 116, 121
Gulistān 59
Gulshan-i rāz 71, **118**
Gulzār-i ma'rifat 23
Gūy va Chaugān (*Ḥāl-nāma*) 122

Ḥadīqat al-ḥaqīqa va-sharī'at aṭ-ṭarīqa 37, **92–94**, 96, 97, 108, 112, 116
Ḥāfiẓ 56, **60–61**, 62, **76–81**, 119, 124
Haft Aurang 123
Haft Paykar 98
hajaz (Persian metre) 14
ḥakīm 44, 86
Ḥāl-nāma see *Gūy va Chaugān*
Ḥālāt va sukhanān-i Shaykh Abū Sa'īd ibn Abī'l-Khayr 16
Ḥallāj, Manṣūr al- 4, 100, 103, 107
Hardy, P. 81
Ḥasan ibn 'Alī (Imam) 93
Ḥasan-i Ghaznavī Ashraf, Sayyid **57, 64**
Ḥaydarī Order 119
Haylāj-nāma 100, 126
Ḥayy ibn Yaqẓān 95
ḥikmat 30, 86
Hilālī 122
Hillmann, M.C. 82
himmat 45
Hoceÿne Azad (Ḥusayn-i Āzād) 23
Hoffmann, B. 126
Hujvīrī 73
Humāy-u Humāyūn 116
Ḥusām ad-Dīn 108, 109, 111
Ḥusayn ibn 'Ali (Imam) 48, 93
Ḥusayn Jalā'irī (Sultan) 61
Ḥusaynī Sādāt Amīr 118
Ḥusn va Dil 122

Iblīs 105
Ibn 'Abbādī 52
Ibn al-'Arabī, Muḥyī ad-Dīn 4, 59, 61, 96, 118
Ibn al-Fāriḍ 4
Ibn al-Munavvar, Muḥammad 16, 23, 24, 75
Ibn al-Muqaffa' 85
Ibn-i Sīnā (Avicenna), Abū 'Alī 12, 89, 95, 101, 123
Ibn-i Yamīn 6
Ibtidā'ī-nāma (*Valad-nāma*) 112
Ilāhī-nāma (by 'Aṭṭar) 12, **102–103**, 108
Ilāhī-nāma (by Sanā'ī) 92
'Imād ad-Dīn Faqīh-i Kirmānī ('Imād-i Faqīh) **60, 119–120**
'Imād ad-Dīn Iṣfahānī 9
Intihā'ī-nāma 113
'Irāqī, Fakhr ad-Dīn **58–59**, 70, 75
'ishq 65, 114
'Ishq-nāma 96
Iskandar-nāma 98
Ismā'īlīs 20, 34, 35, 87
istighnā 101
'itāb 68
I'tiqād-nāma 124
'Izz ad-Dīn Maḥmūd Kāshānī 96

Jājarmī 10, 20
jām-i Jam 76
Jām-i Jam (by Auḥadī) **115–116**
Jamāl ad-Dīn ibn 'Abd ar-Razzāq Iṣfahānī 47, 57

Jāmī, Mullā 'Abd ar-Raḥmān 2, 21, **25, 62, 123–124**
Jamīl ad-Dīn Sāvī 82, 119
Jamshīd 76, 102
Jesus 97, 105
Jones, W. 77
Joseph 22, 123

Kalīla va Dimna 38, 85, 100
Kalimāt al-qiṣār, al- 14, 39
Kamāl ad-Dīn Ismā'īl 47
Kamāl ad-Dīn Mas'ūd Khujandī **61–62**
Kamāl-nāma 117
Karamustafa, A.T. 82
Kārnāma-yi auqāf 118
Kārnāma-yi Balkhī 88
Kātibī of Turshiz 122
Kay-Kā'ūs 31, 78
Kāzarūnī Order 60, 116
khafīf (Persian metre) 96, 112, 116, 117, 124
khalvat 98
Khamsa 98, 116, 123
khānaqāh 37
Khānlarī, P.N. 77
Khāqānī, Afẕal ad-Dīn Ibrāhīm **44–47**, 57, 94, 117
kharābāt 75
Kharaqānī, Abū'l-Ḥasan 13
Kharīdat al-qaṣr 9
Khaṭīb-i Fārisī 82, 119
Khātimat al-ḥayāt 62
Khavātim 59
khirad 30, 86
Khirad-nāma-yi Iskandarī 123
Khiẕr 95, 120
Khulafā' ar-Rāshidūn, al- 32
Khusrau and Shīrīn 66, 98, 116
Khusrau Dihlavī, Amīr **60**, 62, 117
Khusrau-nāma 99
khuṭba 70
Khvājū Kirmānī, Abū'l-'Aṭā Kamāl ad-Dīn Maḥmūd **60, 116–117**, 121
Kisā'ī, Majd ad-Dīn Abū'l-Ḥasan **32–34**
Koran 40, 41, 42, 65, 72, 80, 88, 89, 102, 107, 123
Kunūz al-ḥikma va rumūz al-mutaṣavvifa 38
kushtī 76

Lama 'āt 59, 70
Lavā'iḥ 70
Laylā va Majnūn 123
Lazard, G. 124
Lewis, F.D. 81
Lewisohn, L. 82

ma'ād 89, 115
ma'ānī 44
Ma'ārif 112
ma'āsh 115
mabda' 115
ma'būd 56
madīḥ 29
Maghribī Shīrīn, Maulānā Muḥammad 24, **62**
Maḥmūd of Ghazna (Sultan) 33
majlis 67
Majma' al-baḥrayn 122
Majnūn (Qays) 113
Majnūn and Laylā 66, 98
Makhzan al-asrār **97–98**, 117, 120, 124
malāmat 68, 72, 74, 75, 76
Malāmatīya 72
mamdūḥ 56
manāqib 32, 48

Manāqib al-'ārifīn 108
manāzil 101
Manṭiq aṭ-ṭayr 80, **101–102**, 108
maqāla 97
Maqāmāt aṭ-ṭuyūr see *Manṭiq aṭ-ṭayr*
ma'rifat 101
ma'shūq 56, 65, 78
masnavī **84–127** and *passim*
Masnavī-yi ma'navi **108–111**, 112
Mas'ūd-i Sa'd-i Salmān 49
Maṭla' al-anvār 117
mavā'iẓ 31
Maybūdī, Rashīd ad-Dīn 23, 41
Meer der Seele, Das 100
Meier, F. 27, 81, 83
Meisami, J. Scott 49, 82
Mevlevi Order 108, 109, 111
Michael 105
Miftāḥ al-i 'jāz 71
Mihr va Mushtarī 122
Minorsky, V. 27
Mīnuvī, M. 27
mi'rāj (Ascension to Heaven) 48, 88, 95, 98, 116
Mīrānshāh (Timurid prince) 62
Mir'āt aṣ-ṣafā 45
Mirṣād al-'ibād min al-mabda' ilā'l-ma'ād 10, 23, 71
Miṣbāh al-arvāḥ **95**
Moses 105
Muḥammad ibn Manṣūr, Sayf ad-Dīn 36, 42, 43, 88, 94
Muḥammad, the Prophet 31, 40, 45, 52, 60, 88, 93, 102, 103, 105, 120
Muḥtasham 49
Mukhtār-nāma **21–23**
Mu'nis al-abrār see *Ṣafā-nāma*
Mu'nis al-aḥrār 10, 20, 70
Mu'nis al-'ushshāq 70
muqaṭṭa'a see *qiṭ'a*
muqrī 24
Muṣībat-nama **104–106**, 108, 109, 117
Mustanṣir, al- (Fatimid Caliph) 34
Mutanabbī, al- 30
mutaqārib (Persian metre) 113

Nafaḥāt al-Uns 62
Nafīsī, Sa'īd 20, 28, 99, 125
nafs-i fāniya 95
Najm ad-Dīn Dāya 10, 12, 23, 42, 71
Nakhchavānī, Aḥmad an- 96
Naqshbandī Order 25, 62, 124
Naṣīr ad-Dīn Ṭūsī 20
Nāṣir-i Khusrau **34–35**, 87, 91
Naṣr-Allāh Munshī 38
na't 32, 48
Nicholson, R.A. 5, 18, 27, 45, 81, 82, 109
Nicolas, J.B. 11
Ni'mat-Allāh Valī, Shāh 25, **62**
Ni'mat-Allāhī Order 25
Niẓām ad-Dīn Auliyā 60
Niẓāmī, Ilyās ibn Yūsuf 45, **97–99**, 106, 116, 117, 120, 123, 125, 126
Noah 46, 105
Nūshirvān 97
Nuzhat al-majālis 10

Panchatantram 85
pand-nāmag 86
Panj Ganj 119
pen name see *takhalluṣ*
pīr-i mughān 76
Pothifar 123

Prophet, the see Muḥammad
Pūr-i Bahā 118

Qābūs-nāma 31
qalandar 15, 18, 56, 74, 75, 119
Qalandar-nāma 74
Qalandarīya 74
qalandarīyāt (*qalandarī* poetry) 74–75, 103
qallāsh 75
qanā'at 44
qaṣīda **29–50** and *passim*
Qāsim-i Anvār 25, **62, 120–121**
qavvāl 17
Qays (Majnūn) 98
qiṭ'a (*muqaṭṭa'a*) 6
Qivāmī 47
quatrain see *rubā'ī*

Rabāb-nāma 113
Rābi'a 4, 69
radīf 53, 81
Rāḥat aṣ-ṣudūr 27
Rahman, M. 82
Rashīd ad-Dīn (historian) 116
Raushanā'ī-nāma 87, 91
Rauẓat al-anvār 117
Rāvandī, Muḥammad 27, 42
Raẓavī, M. 125
Reinert, B. 49, 81
Ritter, H. 57, 82, 100, 126
riyā 73, 121
Riyāẓ al-'ārifīn 23
Riẓā-Qulī Khān Hidāyat 13, 23
rubā'i (quatrain) **6–28** and *passim*
Rubā'ī-yi ḥaurā'īya **24**
Rūdakī 7, 85
Rūmī, Maulānā Jalāl ad-Dīn 21, 42, **57–58, 108–11**, 112, 115
Rūzbihān-i Baqlī 96
Rypka, J. 26, 50, 59, 81, 82

Ṣa'ādat-nāma (by Maḥmūd Shabistarī) 118
Ṣa'ādat-nāma (by Nāṣir Khusrau) 87
Ṣad maqām dar iṣṭilāḥ-i ṣūfīya 120
Sa'dī, Musharrif ad-Dīn **59–60**, 61, **113–114**, 115, 119, 121
Ṣadr ad-Dīn Qunavī 59
Ṣafā-nāma (*Mu'nis al-abrār*) 120
Safar-nāma 34
Safavid Order 62
Ṣafī ad-Dīn (Safavid sheikh) 62, 121
Ṣā'ib 63
Ṣalāḥ ad-Dīn Farīdūn Zarkūb 112
Salāmān va Absāl **123**
Salmān-i Sāvajī 60
samā' 17, **69**
Ṣan'ān, Sheikh 79, 80, 103
Sanā'ī, Majdūd ibn Ādam 21, **35–43**, 47, **56**, 57, 58, 61, 87, **88–95**, 96–98, 106, 108, 109, 111, 112, 116, 117, 124
Sanjar (Saljuq Sultan) 97
sāqī 67
Saranjām 14
sarī' (Persian metre) 97
Savāniḥ 23, 59, 74
Sayr al-'ibād ilā'l-ma'ād **88–91**, 93, 95, 106, 109, 117
Schimmel, A. 5, 49, 81, 82, 126
Schmidt, H.-P. 126
Shabistarī, Maḥmūd 71, **118**
shafā'a 106

Shāfi'ī, ash- 93
Shafī'ī-Kadkanī, M.R. 28
Shāh Shujā' (ruler of Shiraz) 119
Shāh va Gadā 122
Shāh-nāma 83, 85, 114
shahāda 40
shāhid 39, 67
Shahriyār, Muḥammad-Ḥusayn 63
Sham' va Parvāna 122
Shams ad-Dīn Tabrīzī (Shams-i Tabrīzī) 42, 58, 109, 111, 112–113
Shams ad-Dīn Lāhijī 71
Shams-i Qays 7
Sharḥ-i rubā'īyāt 25
sharī'at 75
Shehrazade 100
Shīrīn 114
Siḥr-i ḥalāl 122
Silsilat az̲-z̲ahab 124
Sīmurgh 101–103
Solomon 102
Stolz, K. 82
Subḥat al-asrār 124
Ṣuḥbat-nāma **119**
Suhravardī, Shihāb ad-Dīn Abū Ḥafṣ 'Umar 74, 114
Suhravardī, Shihāb ad-Dīn Yaḥyā (al-Maqtūl) 42, 70
Sulṭān Valad 42, 58, **111–113**

takhalluṣ (pen name) 54, 97
Taqīzāda, Ḥ. 49
Ṭarabkhāna 10
tarāna 7
Ṭarīq at-taḥqīq 96
Tarjumān al-ashwāq 4
taṣavvuf 4
taubīkh 68
tauḥīd 32, 48, 101
Ṭayyibāt 59
taz̲kira 23
Taz̲kirat al-auliyā 102
Tholuck, F.A.D. 126
ṭībat al-qalb 73
Tortel, Chr. 106
Traditions 40
Tughril Beg (Saljuq Sultan) 13
Tuḥfat al-aḥrār 124
Tuḥfat al-'Irāqayn 95, 117
Tuḥfat aṣ-ṣighar 60

'Umar (Caliph) 32, 93
'Umar-i Khayyām **9–13**
Unity of Being see *waḥdat al-wujūd*
Ushtur-nāma 100, 125
Utas, B. 125
'Uthmān (Caliph) 32, 93

Valad-nāma (*Ibtidā'ī-nāma*) 112
Vasaṭ al-ḥayāt 60
Vāsiṭat al-'iqd 62
vaṣl 78
va'ẓ 33, 69

Wagner, E. 49
waḥdat al-wujūd (Unity of Being) 4, 25, 59, 61
Wickens, G.M. 82

Yazici, T. 126
Yohannan, J.D. 81
Yūsuf va Zulaykhā 25, 66, 123

zaban-i ḥāl 104, 109
Zād al-musāfirīn 118
Zarrīnkoob, A.H. 50
z̲auq 72

Zhukovsky, V. 10, 28
zuhd 30, 32, 33
zuhdīyāt 30, 31, 38, 41, 43, 45, 48
zunnār 28, 76, 80